LEARNING LATER

Brian Findsen
Auckland University of Technology
and The University of Glasgow

KRIEGER PUBLISHING COMPANY
MALABAR, FLORIDA
2005

Original Edition 2005

Printed and Published by
KRIEGER PUBLISHING COMPANY
KRIEGER DRIVE
MALABAR, FLORIDA 32950

Library of Congress Cataloging-in-Publication Data

Findsen, Brian.
    Learning later / Brian Findsen. — Original ed.
      p. cm.
    Includes bibliographical references and index.
    ISBN 1-57524-218-4 (alk. paper)
    1. Adult learning—Social aspects. 2. Adult education—Social aspects.
    3. Aging—Social aspects. I. Title.
LC5225.L42F56 2005
374—dc22   2004043846

10 9 8 7 6 5 4 3 2

CONTENTS

PREFACE

It is not possible for me to identify a precise moment when I thought I would write a book on older adults and learning. It has been more of a gradual process in which I have accumulated more knowledge of the aging process and reflected on the field of educational gerontology. In this journey there have been some definable moments which have triggered my more intense interest in this subject. These are relevant to share here as the springboard for writing this book. I have separated these influences into more personal motivating factors and those emergent from more societal-wide developments. Quite obviously, there is considerable overlap between the personal and the public.

Personal Influences

First, I have had a long-term interest as an adult educator in New Zealand in the democratization of education. I mean by this that there should be equal opportunities for people of whatever background to have ready access to what we would all consider to be a "good education". I refer here not only to equal educational opportunity (an argument based on the rights of individuals) but also to social equity (the equal access of groups in society to resources, whether education, housing, health etc). The context of New Zealand where this book has been constructed is quite important because most New Zealanders have a strong social justice ethic in a relatively new land distant from the hurly-burly of the Northern Hemisphere. Yet because of colonization, our influences are heavily English or European, supplemented more recently by American and Pasifika peoples.

In addition, ethnic relations between indigenous Maori and Pakeha (European), while historically stormy, have been implemented in a largely consensual bi-cultural framework, respecting the rights of indigenous peoples to self-determination.

My earlier writing has focussed on social equity issues, with strong appeals to concerns of Maori, women and working class people. While I am a male middle-class academic, my own family roots were working class and I have continued to hold what I think of as a healthy skepticism for education processes and the role of institutions, especially universities, in the lives of ordinary people. The recent "massification of education" (Evans & Abbott, 1998) prevalent in most Western tertiary education systems has provided such institutions with direct challenges of dealing effectively with a wide range of people (but that's another story).

As an adult educator who has spent about 20 years in three New Zealand universities of different character and several shorter periods in the USA and the UK, I have had occasion to teach adult education classes to many adults from beginning certificate courses to doctoral level. I have also been a postgraduate student at a North American university in the mid-to-late 1980s and been the recipient of many tertiary teachers' styles of working with mature adult students. Throughout this experiencing of adult teaching-learning processes, I have not veered from an active interest in access and quality of education issues for marginalized groups in society. In particular, this analysis of the differential experiences of nontraditional or minority students has been spurred by my reintroduction to the sociology of education in postgraduate studies at North Carolina State University. I say "re-introduction" because as a novice (freshman) in the early 1970s I studied sociology in my first year of undergraduate study and mentally noted that I would never be a lover of sociology! I was wrong.

While a significant number of older adults are financially secure and part of the mainstream of economic and cultural life, many more are not. In this sense, selected sections of the older adult population are certainly non-traditional and constitute a minority group. Hence, part of my professional interest in adults in the third age is that historically many have been disenfranchised from education in their earlier lives and this pattern has persisted into late adulthood.

Another major factor in my exploration of older adults and learning has been triggered by my own observation of the aging process in myself and in friends and relatives. As a sometime teacher of adult development theory in classes, I have thought about how "stage", "phase" and "life transitions" theory apply to myself. Now in my early 50s, I have been much more reflective of how I spend my time and the limitations and opportunities which come my way, partially as a result of my consciousness of aging. I have a continuing interest in the extent to which constraints in older life are "real" and/or those that are socially induced (via societal expectations).

In early 1999 I was able to spend time at the University of Georgia, Athens, as a visiting academic in the Department of Adult Education. This provided me with the chance to talk with people who taught in this area of educational gerontology but, just as importantly, the opportunity to read in this area and build up a better theoretical knowledge base. Subsequently, I spent a couple of months in Southern England and visited academics, historians, practitioners, and organizations associated with older adults' learning (e.g. U3A, Age Concern, the Pre-Retirement Association, the National Institute of Adult Continuing Education) throughout the UK to consolidate my understanding of practice in (social) gerontology.

In that same year (1999—the International Year of Older Persons), I was fortunate to "represent" New Zealand at a Singaporean-based conference focussing on older adults' education organized by the Asia South Pacific Bureau of Adult Education (ASPBAE). This conference which attracted "leaders" in the field from respective countries (Singapore, China, Japan, India, Malaysia, South Korea, Australia, New Zealand) focussed on issues of older adults' learning. Participants pledged commitment to future investigations first through research in their home countries then subsequently cross-nationally. What became obvious at this conference was the paucity of research and studies in the area of educational gerontology and the need for both theoretical and practical work at a local and international context. I have committed myself to theoretical investigation of this emerging field and to empirical research currently underway.

The Singaporean conference, just described, was an indicator of the heightened interest in the plight of older adults internationally in the third age. As educators and practitioners working with older adults, it has been natural to ask educational questions such as "What does learning mean for older adults in their lives?" "What kind of learning is occurring for older adults?" "What access do they have to educational provision?" "What counts as knowledge for seniors, for governments, for policy-makers?" and so on. The questions have kept coming. It's time for more answers.

A final professional factor in this decision to write a book came from my teaching a master's level course in 2000 at the University of Auckland on "Learning in Later Life". Preparation for this course required lots of reading and the compilation of a reader consisting of articles from adult learning, educational gerontology and social gerontology. The thought of having a book available which would be better attuned to the learning needs of mature-age students in the program was appealing.

Societal Influences

The turn of economic and political events in the last couple of decades in most Western countries has drawn attention to the importance of learning for life. Most governments have realized that they cannot afford to ignore the potential of older adults as part of a revamped workforce but also as mentors for the next generations. "Lifelong learning", "the learning society", "the knowledge wave" are all terms which are in much more common usage by politicians, business-people and laypersons alike. Third age learners, now much more conspicuous, have potentially more voting influence and political power than in the past. Their social needs, including learning needs, can no longer be neglected by a government wanting to be returned to office. The time is ripe for pushing the cause of lifelong learning, with people in the third age an undeniable force as advocates.

The more recent incorporation of lifelong learning ideas into public policy at a variety of levels (local authorities, state or county level, national governments) has lead to the questioning of the rights of all citizens to education, regardless of age, gender, ethnicity or social class. This recent interest has not been accidental. In the New Zealand context (and probably in many other Western nations), the rhetoric of government has been to increase the capacity of the workforce through up-skilling and to establish a sounder knowledge base in order to be internationally competitive. In other words, there is an economic driver to the creation of a "learning society". Whatever the motives, there is undoubtedly a revitalization of the need for lifelong education so that people do not lose their knowledge currency as knowledge can quickly become obsolete (Naisbitt, 1984; Toffler, 1980).

This book should be of use to older adults themselves to reflect on their own learning experiences, to practicing professionals to illuminate their interactions with older adults, and to students in a variety of settings—health, adult education, social work, volunteering, management and caring professions (e.g. nursing). Although it is written using a theoretical and research base, it is intended for practitioners in search of constructive ways of conceptualizing their work with older adults and of pragmatic ways forward.

ACKNOWLEDGMENTS

First, I would like to express my gratitude to Catherine, my wife, who has provided consistent support for my academic career and the writing of this book, in particular. We sacrificed time together so that this project could come to fruition.

A whole host of people in casual conversation and in more earnest dialogue has influenced the direction and content of this book. I wish to identify especially the Singaporean conference of November 1999, the colleagues I met there, as a springboard to undertake this work. More recently members of the Older Persons and Adult Learning (OPAL) Network Auckland have motivated me to complete this publication. In addition, the multitude of postgraduate students and colleagues has assisted my thinking about older adults' learning. There is still so much more to learn.

Finally, towards the end of this project I worked alongside Lucila Carvalho and Koshila Kumar, research officers at the School of Education, Auckland University of Technology, to hasten its completion. I appreciated their fine research capabilities and ongoing goodwill.

CHAPTER 1

Introduction

In the last decade, at least, there has been a growing global awareness of the demographic changes in most nation-states in which there are growing numbers of older adults in proportion to other age cohorts within the lifecourse. Coupled with this demographic phenomenon has been an increase in the life expectancy of humans brought about primarily by technological advances in health care. So, for the first time in human history, there will be large numbers of older adults living what Peter Laslett (1989) has called "the third age" in *A Fresh Map of Life*.

The area of educational gerontology, as described in the next chapter, has had a spotty history as theorists and practitioners alike have sought to better comprehend the nature of older adults' learning. The domain of the third age has definite challenges for educators—for example, how to understand the life expectations and educational aspirations of this growing sector in most societies; how to effectively collaborate with older adults to help them plan and implement their learning goals; how to mobilize educational providers to take the desires of older adults for learning more seriously. Within educational gerontology, much of the literature has emphasized the "educational needs" of older adults in isolation from social context. The allied field of adult education has so far established some insights into older adults' pedagogy from a "how to" perspective but has been rather devoid of tough theoretical analysis of older adults' learning. These fields have not really explored beneath the surface of older adults' educational need to understand their underlying social, political and economic positioning which, I argue in this book, has greater explanatory power than the prevailing psychological explanations of older adults and learning.

LIFELONG LEARNING AND EDUCATION
IN THE THIRD AGE

While the difference between "lifelong learning" and "life-long education" will be disentangled later in this book, an essential point about these notions is that societies are looking at continuity of learning through individuals' lives. Schooling is no longer an adequate preparation for life (if it ever was)—it is part of a lifelong learning journey where the state has invested resources early in an individual's basic education. Importantly, in terms of the parameters of this book, lifelong learning necessitates attention to older adults in a variety of social roles, even if most attention is given to economic and employment issues by the state rather than in fuller participation of older adults as citizens.

As will be discussed in more detail in chapter 4, there has been a change in emphasis, perhaps gradual in some countries, away from the trajectory of the individual's lifecourse of initial education, to work and adult responsibilities to "retirement" and leisure. Instead, there is a more complex, but exciting move, to conceptualizing education, work and leisure operating in an integrated system (Riley & Riley, 1994). The effect of this social change is to uphold principles of adult learning throughout life beyond schooling to include the circumstances of older adults.

The intention of this book is to explore the social dimensions and educational implications of the new "third age" phenomenon. A basic underlying assumption is that it is necessary to understand the educational aspirations and demands of older adults in terms of their social and material conditions. In this case, the emphasis is placed on those conditions experienced in Western cultures (while acknowledging the wider international character of living and learning in the third age). The objective is to incorporate an understanding of older adults' learning from two main perspectives: from that of adult learning theory applied to older adults; from that of social gerontology which clarifies the social issues faced by this sector of the community. In effect, the book provides an integration of these perspectives so that older adults' learning is grasped from a more analytical and holistic framework. In addition, it also provides practitioners with suggestions of how to respond to issues raised throughout the chapters.

I argue that while applying adult learning perspectives conveys some understanding of why and how older adults learn, it is too restrictive since the depictions from adult learning theory are quite generic and so often divorced from gender, social class and ethnic identity issues. Social gerontologists, especially the "critical gerontologists", help fill this gap by providing insights into structural constraints faced by older learners in their daily lives. Hence, the content for this book is a blend of adult learning theory applied to older adults together with critical perspectives from social gerontological literature and practice. This is a new approach being offered, with a stronger emphasis on the social gerontological dimensions than the adult learning perspective, though they should not be separated.

My impression is that the application of adult learning theory to older adults does help us understand their learning processes *to a degree* but this is insufficient in itself to explain the complexities of this learning. As a sociologist of (adult) education, I assert that little in "pure" adult learning theory prepares us for the contradictions, tensions and paradoxes of aging. Essentially, aging is not just a physiological or even psychological process; it is fundamentally socially constructed (Berger and Luckmann, 1991) and must be understood, in part at least, by considering the broader cultural, political, economic and social circumstances in which older adults find themselves. Hence, the need to discover how social gerontology (concerned as it is with the social processes and structures of older adults) can contribute to a fuller understanding of older adults' learning.

In this book a range of theories and perspectives are presented concerning older adults' lives and their learning. This includes functionalist (essentially a more conservative positioning), interpretive and radical perspectives from sociology to encapsulate a range of explanations from that discipline. In particular, the political economy approach, much favored in this text, is derivative of a more left-wing macro perspective within the conflict theory approach in sociology. From within "critical theory" (or more accurately, groups of critical theories), I use the more specific field of "critical gerontology" (essentially critical theory applied to gerontology) to elucidate the dynamics of older adults' contexts and educational aspirations. Within this array of perspectives is the underlying message that we can understand older adults' learning from a multitude of viewpoints but fuller understanding emerges from those perspectives which emphasize critical and social dimensions.

My argument is that it is through investigating the social context of older adults' lives that we come to understand what meaningful learning is to them. Phrased another way, if we study the social lives of older adults, what they do in their daily lives, then we will see how learning is derived from the complex issues and concerns they face. This provides us with a fuller context for their learning. This book is structured to investigate both the social contexts of older adults' lives and the kinds of learning that they do.

The Structure of This Book

I have structured the book so that in the earlier sections, apart from an initial introduction to educational gerontology, the emphasis is placed on the social contexts of older adults. Thereafter, I present chapters dealing with more explicit educational issues, followed by a consideration of social issues facing older adults. In effect, this order of presentation constitutes an interweaving of the social and the educational, a metaphor which matches the overall intent of the book. The final chapter returns to a more educational theme in exploring what a "critical educational gerontology" can contribute to our understanding of third age learning.

Chapter 2 provides a framework for understanding the emerging field of educational gerontology. An early distinction is made between "education" of older adults and the "learning" which they may undertake. It is argued that if we look at learning then most older people engage in informal and nonformal modes, if not in formalized learning environments. I also discuss who *is* an older adult and the problems of definition. Just as adult education has numerous underlying philosophies (Elias & Merriam, 1995), so too does educational gerontology. A brief history of the development of educational gerontology is provided before looking at how it connects with the notion of lifelong learning. It is suggested that a "critical" educational gerontology will best allow older adults to assert their interests, inclusive of their learning imperatives. This theme is later revisited in the final chapter after a fuller context of third age learning has been discussed.

In chapters 3 and 4 the wider context of aging and the challenges presented by social change for older adults are analyzed. In chapter 3 a range of theories from multiple disciplines is offered to explain different aspects of the aging process. In particular, a clear demarcation is drawn between functionalist arguments of aging, which tend to present a deficit depiction of aging and older adults, and more liberating perspectives. Over a few decades adult developmental theorists have presented varied pictures of older adulthood and several of these are discussed, including life transitions approaches. In the latter section of this chapter sociological viewpoints of aging are debated—age stratification, labeling, subcultural and social phenomenological. These tend to emphasize the impact of social structures on older adults (determinism) or the relative autonomy and choices open to elders (agency). The intent is not to discount the value of earlier constructions of aging (e.g. functionalism) but to point to the greater explanatory power from more critical sociological perspectives.

To stress that aging is a dynamic process, I have included discussion on social change, including historical and cultural images of what older age might mean in varying contexts. Popular images of older adulthood are presented and myths concerning the characteristics of third age people are analyzed and debunked. Discrimination against different subordinate groups of older adults is evident in all societies, usually related to a group's position in the political economy. The role of the state (government and its ministries) and education institutions connected with the state are discussed because these can have a significant effect on people in the third age, as exemplified by structural dependency. Two more aspects of social change are discussed in relation to the political economy—the institution of retirement which is differentially experienced by different subgroups of older adults; the issue of gender and aging, given that older age is often described as a feminized phenomenon.

In the next two chapters the focus is placed upon the participation of older adults in learning/education, and what agencies do to facilitate educational gerontology. In chapter 5 the issue of (non) participation of people in education in the third age is addressed. It is not a pleasant story, especially if you belong to a nontraditional group. Participation in mainstream older adult education has been quite strongly captured by the white middle-class, who have already benefited well from the system. I provide some insight into the barriers encountered by older adults and present arguments for equal access of education to any person in the third age. The heterogeneity of people in the third age is a distinguishing characteristic—there are many different groups of older adults who possess different forms of *cultural capital* (Bourdieu, 1974). While we can advocate for justice in terms of access to education, the kind of learning chosen by groups tends to reflect their relative positions in the social structure and their cultural heritage. This is why a political economy approach is so valued—it positions the learning of older adults within their economic and social circumstances, largely determined by social stratification according to social class, gender, race/ethnicity, geographical location, (dis)ability etc.

If we examine the provision of formal organized learning for older adults by educational providers, the situation internationally is rather dismal. Before discussing types of agencies involved in adult education provision, it is first necessary to understand the wider field of which third age education is a part. (Educational provision for older adults seldom exists in isolation from more general provision, though there are exceptions). Although formal provision is fragmented and philosophically diverse, it is not only *education* agencies that have a role in providing learning opportunities for elders. Hence, I explore other agencies that provide for third age learners, usually as a subsidiary social function.

Harry Moody (1976), from a humanist tradition of educational gerontology, has put forward a thematic approach with respect to different categories of modal patterns of behavior directed towards or enacted by older adults—rejection, social service, participation and self-actualization. The first two patterns illustrate the relative invisibility and powerlessness of older adults linked to their perceived dependency on the rest of society. These patterns of how older adults have customarily been treated within society have equivalence in educational practice. The latter two patterns are emphasized later in this book as more useful patterns from which older adults can exercise greater self-determination in their lives. In the closing section of chapter 6, I introduce several older adult educational institutions— the University of the Third Age (U3A) as an exemplar of a successful self-help agency whose control is firmly in the hands of older learners themselves—and American inspired programs of Elderhostel and Institutes of Learning in Retirement (ILRs). Then issues commonly faced by education providers are discussed with a view to suggesting fruitful ways forward.

Given that older adults live much of their lives in social institutions, it is incumbent to ask what impact such institutions have on third age learners. These institutions of education, work and leisure (to use Riley and Riley's model of integrated structures) provide rich opportunities for older adults to develop social relationships and gain further knowledge, usually in an informal way. In chapter 7 I explore learning in different institutions—the family, the church, the media, community settings and the world of work. Each of these social situations proffers considerable prospects of learning for analysis. In addition, the issues of intergenerational learning and volunteering are included because both of these modes of social activity are packed with potential for learning across social groups and generations.

Part of the fascination of studying older adult education from a social gerontological position is that learning emerges from issues with which third age learners are directly engaged or influenced by. In the penultimate chapter the issues of struc-

tural lag, independence or interdependence, technological innovation, cultural variation in aging, dealing with death and dying
and social policy challenges for nations are discussed. These issues have been selected somewhat arbitrarily but mainly because
they have been to the fore in older people's lives across nations.
The novel approach taken in this book is to more explicitly connect these issues with the potential for learning of older adults.

The final chapter draws together strands from previous
ones but concentrates on presenting a way forward both theo-
retically and pragmatically. Initially the question of what a critical educational gerontology can offer educators and other practitioners in a theoretical sense is discussed. At the heart of this
debate is the issue of empowerment for older adults which links
with earlier discussion of a critical perspective. I then use the
critical (radical) approach of political economy as illustrative of
how a critical perspective can enhance our analysis of older
adults' learning and point to fruitful ways in which to better
comprehend the dynamics of oppressed groups of people (including significant subpopulations of seniors). In pointing the
way for the future, I recommend that as practitioners we need
to better understand the viewpoints of older adults (looking in-
wards) in the fuller social context of their lives (looking out-
wards). We need to better integrate theory and practice in educational gerontology—theory that informs practice and arises
from practice; practice that is influenced by stronger theoretical
understandings derived from the convergence of adult learning
theory and social gerontology.

CHAPTER 2

Conceptions of Educational Gerontology

In this chapter a range of terms and concepts related to the education of older adults are explored to provide greater clarity on this interdisciplinary area and to provide some understanding of the underlying issues beneath the surface of educational gerontology. Initially, I explore different modes of learning for older adults then address the problematic of just who are older adults. A discussion of philosophies of education pertaining to older adults is next provided as a preliminary to the historical development of the field of educational gerontology. Importantly, the links between this emerging field with the concept of lifelong learning are delineated prior to discussing the idea of a critical educational gerontology (subsequently elaborated upon in the final chapter). Overall, it should be stressed that little knowledge is settled conceptually in this area and this book has been constructed to explore connections between the social contexts of older adults' lives and their learning and to contribute to a broader understanding of this dynamic field of human endeavor.

The term *educational gerontology* has been in existence for a few decades though its meaning has varied over time and from place to place. In some ways, this label has been used as a synonym for "older adult education" but usually it has been more expansive in what it purports to include. Before the term educational gerontology can be adequately unraveled, it is necessary to register that even the phrases "education" and "learning" are not self-evident in their meaning. One of the fundamental positions taken in this book is that we need to concentrate more upon learning and less upon education if we are to fully comprehend the rich dimensions of people's lives, including those of older adults. Research continually demonstrates (e.g. Sargent, 1997) that the participation levels of older adults in education (organized, structured learning) is not as high as national norms for adult participation yet the diversity of learning activities among older adults is considerable (Hiemstra, 1976). We need to know more about not only educational participation of older adults per se (i.e. understanding education structures and provider profiles) but also the myriad other forms of learning in which they engage.

As Jarvis (1985, p.3) has pointed out, there are three contexts for learning:

> *Informal learning*—the process whereby every person acquires knowledge, skills, attitudes and aptitude from daily living;
> *Nonformal learning*—any systematic, organized, educational activity carried on outside the formal system to provide selected types of learning to particular subgroups of the population;
> *Formal learning*—the institutionalized, chronologically graded and hierarchical educational system.

For virtually everyone the first category occurs incidentally in daily life with little conscious thought to the process. The work undertaken by Canadian Allen Tough (1971) is significant. He investigated the character of adults' learning where he attempted to gain insights into how much time and effort adults invested in *learning projects*—i.e. a major learning effort which is a deliberate and sustained (minimum of 7 hours) attempt to gain some clear knowledge or skill. Tough was able to demonstrate "that 'the average adult' spends about 90–100 hours on each learning project, conducts eight such projects every year, and plans or directs the projects personally" (Tennant, 1988, p.10). An application of this kind of approach to a study of older adults learning patterns would help us understand more about what they do outside of usual educational structures. In particular, an analysis of working class and minority groups' learning projects would be especially useful.

The second category is one in which many older adults would engage. Nonformal learning contexts for older adults are plentiful. Many older adults are members of recreational groups, arts organizations, social welfare agencies, community learning centers or voluntary organizations in which they play major roles. In some instances, such as the University of the Third Age (U3A), learning activity is the primary task of members. In grandparent roles, too, older adults may be active players in intergenerational programs, significant for their own personal learning and for the learning of the wider community. Nonformal learning, as explained in more detail in chapter 7, constitutes a very significant portion of older people's lives and promotion of such activity by practitioners is time very well spent.

The third category may consist of tertiary education providers such as universities, community colleges and other environments in which there is a clear hierarchical structure, often related to credentialism and usually more vocationally oriented. Not many older adults participate in such learning contexts (Carlton & Soulsby, 1999) because they often prefer more expressive forms of learning and they may have longstanding inhibitions about entering formal education based on their own schooling experiences (Pearce, 1991). Formal learning contexts sometimes evoke fear, performance anxiety and expectations of passivity (Cross, 1981). It is incumbent upon practitioners working with older adults to help demystify educational institutions and to help build better bridges between these providers of learning opportunities and older people's daily living routines.

In this book *learning* is used in its widest sense, synonymous with its informal character i.e. a process employed by adults to acquire knowledge, skills, attitudes and aptitudes (Darkenwald & Merriam, 1982). The issue of inequalities in participation, while applicable to all forms of learning, is primarily targeted at formal learning (education), where older adults often have been disenfranchised.

WHO ARE OLDER ADULTS?

When we speak of older adults' learning, what is meant by *older adults*? While there is a huge literature, especially in the USA, on older adults and educational gerontology, there is no definitive characteristic to distinguish a person as "an older adult". While it may be true to say that "we are as old as we feel" there is, nevertheless, a physical reality that we face some physiological decline as we age which impacts on our daily lives (Beatty & Wolf, 1996). However, we do not have to agree with deficit explanations of aging—those that depict older adults as decrepit, frail or physically and mentally wanting. A more active and positive image of older adulthood can be projected instead. Just as significant to older adults' well-being are personal and societal expectations of what might be appropriate behaviors for them—these can be enhancing or inhibitory. (These stereotypes are investigated more fully in chapter 4).

Defining older adulthood has been problematic. Using chronological age is misleading and dangerous as a criterion because of cultural variations in the social construction of "old age" and huge individual developmental variation within same culture age groups. Neugarten (1976) has formulated a useful categorization which differentiates between *young-old* (adults usually aged 55–65) and the *old-old* (aged 75–85) to distinguish between healthy, active older adults and those less active due to chronic and acute health conditions. Sheehy (1995) points out that what seemingly older adults do now—Neugarten's young-old—are what middle-agers used to do. Many older adults are breaking away from previous social norms and developing their own innovative practices, especially the "baby boomers" (Glendenning, 2000).

Laslett (1989), one of the most influential figures in "the third age" movement in the UK, has identified four ages to describe the dominant periods in an individual's life course. The *first age* is that of childhood and early socialization in which a person is dependent on others; the *second age* is that of adult maturity characterized by an individual's pursuit of career and financial gain. At this point, typically, people will be concerned with forming their own families and taking responsibility for others. In the *third age*, an individual usually exercises fuller autonomy in self-fulfillment, having been released from the trammels of the second age. Often a person can develop more cultural interests and seek enhanced life satisfaction. The *fourth age*, is one of final dependency, decrepitude and death.

Laslett's depiction of older adults in the third age is essentially humanistic and optimistic. He believes that in the 21st century third agers will prosper as larger numbers enter this domain of life with plenty of energy for and creativity in living. However, sooner or later, we all must die. What people desire is a fourth age which has dignity and caring as central components. Educators are guilty of largely ignoring this fourth age yet there is a useful role here for the sensitive care of those who can no longer care properly for themselves. As further developed in chapter 8, the education of carers, both familial and institutional, is an important aspect of coping with grief and loss.

In this work I concentrate upon the third age and its interconnections with learning but through a critical lens.

PHILOSOPHIES OF OLDER ADULTS' EDUCATION

Philosophical approaches to the education of older adults have tended to draw on the same diverse traditions as the field of adult education. The field of adult education itself is multifaceted and varies in its character from place to place. In the American context, Hiemstra (1998, pp.5–6) describes the field as including "Americanisation efforts, literacy programs, vocational training, rural education, cooperative extension, university extension, community education, military education, religious education, and training or human resource development". He points out that educational programming aimed at older adults as a separate entity has been scant and largely unrecorded. Hence, we are left with a fragmented and spotty picture of what is now more often called educational gerontology. For a more elaborate view of the establishment of educational gerontology in the American context, readers are referred to Hiem-stra's article in the Jossey-Bass *New Directions in Adult and Continuing Education* series related to older adulthood (Hiem-stra, 1998).

Returning to the philosophical diversity of the education of older adults, this fragmentation, in part, reflects the differ-ent goals of adults, varying understandings of what constitutes knowledge, and the sheer divergence in groups of people. An example of an orthodox approach to the education of older adults was adopted by Lowy and O'Connor (1986) who used the familiar typology of Elias and Merriam's (1995) five philoso-phies of adult education—liberalism, progressivism, behaviorism, radicalism and humanism—and opted for the last-mentioned as the most appropriate for older adults. While they note that each philosophy has some relevance in providing a rationale for older adult learning, they feel that *humanism*—with its emphasis on freedom, autonomy, individual growth and self-actualization—is the most apposite. This focus on the *expressive* rather than the *instrumental* character of older adults' learning provides an optimistic view of human nature analogous to Laslett's roman-tic ideal of third age learning. The positive feature of this por-trayal of older adults' engagement with learning is that it em-phasizes human agency, the creative and exploratory nature of living, rather than a passive, domesticating construction of older adulthood.

A familiar way for adult educators to determine appropri-ate strategies for educating older adults is to employ the *needs-based* approach. Such approaches, while prevalent in adult edu-cation because of their emphasis of "starting where the learner is at", are fraught with ethical questions (Benseman, 1980; Col-lins, 1991). In the work of prominent humanist adult educator, Malcolm Knowles, his program planning design was closely aligned to the need for educators to assess the learning needs of participants, before and during learning events (Knowles, 1980; Knowles et al., 1984). When this needs-based model is applied to older adult learners, there are several emergent ethical issues to be resolved. For example, who should decide on older adults' learning needs? Usually, the expected answer to this question is the older adults themselves but are they always in the best position to make these decisions and what of other stakeholders' interests (e.g. family members; the state)? Whose needs should predominate and why? Beneath the surface of a needs-based approach resides a rich array of such ethical issues, many of which are ignored by pragmatists. Practitioners should be more conscious of the ethical character of what they do and present educational options of varying moral dimensions with integrity.

A pioneer in studying the learning needs of older adults was McClusky (1974) who distinguished between different kinds of needs which could reasonably be met within the realm of education:

- **coping** needs: adults engaged in physical fitness, economic self-sufficiency, basic education;
- **expressive** needs: adults taking part in activities for their own sake and not necessarily to achieve a goal;
- **contributive** needs: adults deciding how to be useful contributors to society;
- **influence** needs: adults becoming agents for social change.

Many programs organized by adult education agencies might be analyzed according to which of these needs are prominent or which combination of these needs is relevant. (This approach is further discussed in chapter 6). Suffice to say here that the "needs" approach to adult learning reflects the largely pragmatic endeavor that the field of adult education entails but it is subject to critique from critical theorists for its neglect of a moral dimension (Collins, 1991).

THE DEVELOPMENT OF EDUCATIONAL GERONTOLOGY

The phrase "educational gerontology" emerged out of the education for older adults movement and was described by David Peterson, an early American pioneer, as "a field of study and practice that has recently developed at the interface of adult education and social gerontology" (1980, p.62). He further suggested that this new field at that time embrace:

1. education for older adults;

2. public education about aging;

3. the education of professionals and paraprofessionals in the field of ageing.

Both the fields of adult education and of social gerontology are large themselves, the latter really encompassing the fields of study necessary to understand the social aspects of aging such as psychology, sociology, biology, medicine and social work. By definition, social gerontology is a multidisciplinary field. In a classic text entitled *Ageing in Society*, Bond, Coleman and Peace (1998, p.19) further explain that:

> Each discipline brings its own theoretical perspectives and methods—They make assumptions, use concepts in different ways, pose different questions and arrive at different explanations of the ageing process. The perspectives are not right or wrong, simply different.

Getting to grips with educational gerontology requires inclusion of a social dimension, just as an exploration of the subject "Education" does in any respectable University School of Education program. Education has normally included scrutiny from allied disciplines such as psychology, history, philosophy, sociology and economics. Educational gerontology has come to be examined from similar multidisciplinary frameworks—in this book, the social and critical dimensions of this subfield are given prominence.

One of the definitional problems has been in differentiating between *educational gerontology* and *gerontological education*. According to Glendenning (2000, p.80), the former is "concerned with the education and learning potential of older adults including all relevant aspects and processes" or "education in the later years" while the latter is "concerned with education about the realities of an ageing society; and the training of those who wish to work for and among older people, whether they be professional, paraprofessional or acting in a voluntary capacity". Sometimes the term *teaching gerontology* is used for gerontological education. To complicate matters even more, educational gerontology has sometimes reverted to cover all aspects of both terms.

A more detailed distinction between educational gerontology (learning in later years) and gerontological education (teaching gerontology) is available through Glendenning's writings but here it should suffice to delineate the following:

Educational gerontology consists of:

1. instructional gerontology e.g. how older people function; memory and intelligence; learning aptitude

2. senior adult education e.g. enabling older adults to extend their range of knowledge through reflection; curriculum development

3. self-help instructional gerontology e.g. learning and helping others to learn in self-help mode; relationships in a learning group

4. self-help senior adult education e.g. learning groups; peer counselling.

Gerontological education consists of:

5. social gerontology and adult education e.g. stereotypes and myths of older people; tutor training

6. advocacy gerontology e.g. consciousness-raising; discrimination; old people as a mainstream resource in society

7. professional gerontology e.g. professional training of skilled tutors and practitioners; course evaluation

8. gerontology education e.g. post-professional training; training of volunteers; community strategies.
   (Glendenning, 2000, pp.80–83)

Obviously, the interdisciplinary character of educational gerontology makes the above distinctions rather arbitrary but the above eight domains do point to the need to integrate theory and practice across many facets of human endeavour for older adults. Practitioners' familiarity with the distinctions of different sectors of educational gerontology enables them to better focus on what is important and present better arguments for allocation of resources in that subfield.

LIFELONG LEARNING

Another issue to be explored is how educational gerontology connects with the concept of *lifelong learning* which many nations in the world are currently employing in their policy proclamations. How does attention to the education of older adults relate to education throughout the lifecourse?

In recent times governments have made more explicit comments on the importance of lifelong learning as part of their commitment to keeping economies internationally competitive and workers more knowledgeable and skilled in their workplaces (see, for instance, in New Zealand, the statements in Goff's *Learning for Life: two*). Within adult education, the concept of lifelong learning has held a treasured place and its importance to society has largely been self-evident to adult educators. Faure et al. (1972) trumpeted the central role of lifelong learning for people to enjoy fruitful lives in their manifold adult roles—as parents, workers, volunteers, grandparents, caregivers, co-learners. From within this report, at least three central concepts are perceived as fundamental to lifelong learning: "vertical integration", "horizontal integration", and the democratizing of the education system in the name of a learning society. For the purposes of this discussion, vertical integration is significant i.e. the idea of continuing to learn throughout life in all its phases (lifelong learning). This is as important for older adults as for young children. This is coupled with horizontal integration i.e. acknowledging the equal status of learning derived from formal, informal and nonformal contexts (life-wide learning).

In the policy documents of most Western countries, the emphasis has been placed on vocational education and training. It is assumed that the concept of lifelong learning applies to full-time workers rather than older adults, most of whom have re-tired from the paid workforce, at least on a full-time basis. Withnall (2000, pp.88–89) points to the British experience of three major policy reports related to lifelong learning in the UK (Kennedy, 1997; National Committee of Inquiry into Higher Education, 1997; Fryer, 1997) doing little justice to the treatment of noneconomic, personal and social benefits of lifelong learning. The instrumental purposes of education take precedence over the expressive. She concludes this analysis by commenting:

> Indeed, older people are frequently marginalised in educational policy circles by continued emphasis on economic competitiveness in tandem with a moral panic about the financial support of an ageing population which, although of major importance, tends to conceptualise later life as primarily a social problem (Withnall, 2000, p.89)

At a philosophical level, how does the education of older adults fit into a lifelong learning paradigm (assuming it should)? The issue of why should society be bothered about the provision of education to older adults (given their likely imminent death and perceived limited utility to the wider society) should not be avoided. Responses to this question are important for practitioners, policy-makers and researchers alike.

One response to the above challenge is to argue for the ways in which education can enhance the quality of life of all citizens, including older adults. It can be argued that education will contribute towards better life satisfaction, better health and mental well-being. (If an economic argument is needed to run alongside this perspective, then we could measure the extent of increased participation levels of older adults in the workforce and voluntary activities and of the cost savings in medical care). In Australia, particularly through the work of Richard Swindell at Griffith University on the positive impact of the U3A movement on the quality of life of older adults (1997), this cost-benefit approach has been adopted.

Another, perhaps more persuasive approach, is to argue for the rights of older adults to equality of treatment i.e. to use an equality of educational opportunity position. This approach has been used to good effect in the UK. Schuller and Bostyn's (1992) enquiry into third age learning argued for educational entitlement for all adults. In addition, their argument was strengthened by including a compensatory clause—most older adults in British society have contributed taxes throughout their lives and received comparatively few opportunities in their youth (especially given the stark divides of gender and social class as factors contributing to differential opportunity). It is a matter of social justice that educational opportunities be available to older adults. This position has been sustained in recent work through the National Institute for Adult and Continuing Education's (NIACE) *Older and Bolder* project which is essentially a policy document reinforcing older people's rights to education.

In another approach, very similar to the educational opportunity argument, is that assumed by Withnall and Percy (1994) and Elmore (2000). Withnall and Percy advocate for an emphasis on human dignity and human potential, wherein age is irrelevant as a basis for an effective contribution to society. Elmore (2000) argues for active democratic participation and equality of status in citizenship for older adults—in this way, educational gerontology may become a valuable tool of liberal democracy.

Withnall (2000) makes another argument to support the education of older adults. She refers to the *1993 European Year of Older People and Solidarity Between Generations* as a springboard for discussions on the role of grandparents as participants in family learning based on intergenerational recognition and reciprocity. The theme of generativity is alive and well in much of the work, especially in the USA, on practical intergenerational activities. At a conceptual level, such work relates to adult developmental theory, much of which relies on arguing for "stages" through which adults progress (e.g. Erikson et al., 1978; Levinson et al., 1978). As the diversity of life experiences and transitions among older adults increases, the strength of this theoretical base for intergenerational work diminishes. (This adult developmental approach is further discussed in chapter 3).

A NEW APPROACH TO
EDUCATIONAL GERONTOLOGY

In the field of educational gerontology (or "older adults and learning", as I prefer to call it), the predominant preoccupation has been describing what *is* rather than what *could* or *ought to be*. Studies of older adults have tended to emphasize how this population of adults can achieve "successful aging", as if there is some golden future available to all, if only they knew the right formula to achieve it—good exercise, sensible diet, mental alertness, social participation, continuing education etc. This line of thinking is further influenced by populists such as Peter Laslett whose romanticized view of older age holds sway in many educational gerontologists' quarters. Laslett's is not an entirely inaccurate perspective—it's just that it is not realistically attainable for the vast majority of seniors who live in a myriad of social and material conditions, some quite depressing.

Sociologists label this approach of upholding the status quo as the *functionalist* position. Essentially functionalists argue for examining the roles of people in social systems, of disentangling a social network and asking "What is the function of this person or group?" Applying this perspective to older adults stresses the importance of such elements as role theory and the disengagement hypothesis. Retirement, for example, becomes a matter of adjusting men and women to a new daily regime, of modifying the individual to society's requirements. This argument is consistent with a liberal ideology of education of self-improvement and individual advancement. Such a conservative approach does little to further the interests of older adults who are marginalized and struggle to exercise any real influence over their lives.

In a critique of conventional wisdom in educational gerontology, Glendenning and Battersby (1990, pp.223–25) point to then current inadequacies of educational gerontology and to future challenges. These criticisms and challenges are summarized as follows:

1. The need to argue against the tendency to consider the elderly as one homogeneous group as if social class, gender and ethnicity differences can be easily erased by participation in education.

2. The admission that the plethora of psychologically driven research into developmental, cognitive and learning characteristics of older adults has presented a confusing picture which tends to emphasize their deficits.

3. The recognition that there is very little that education can do to reverse any declines in the physiological condition of older adults.

4. The dearth of philosophical debate on the purposes of education for older adults i.e. why older adults should continue to be educated.

5. Educational provision for older adults has been driven by middle-class notions of "education". This has created a pretentiousness which should be challenged.

6. In the political climate of the New Right, the call for "education for older people" has really just slogan status and we are fooling ourselves to think differently.

7. The question of "Whose interests are being served?" needs to be continually asked since there is now in existence a major exploitative industry which purports to meet the learning needs of older adults.

This critique was constructed over a decade ago, and much of it still holds true though perhaps with some changes of emphasis. These authors' views are presented here to illustrate that debate rages within many issues in educational gerontology. It is my belief that critical discussion of this type is positive and useful. Ultimately, however, any criticism should be matched by constructive steps to be taken for the future.

Hence, this book supports a critical approach and argues

for a more hardened coupling of adult learning theory with so-cial gerontology as an appropriate way forward (Bury, 1995; Estes, 1991). In the final chapter of this book I discuss the fuller ramifications of using a critical theory approach to educational gerontology. Next, I draw together the main strands of this chapter.

CONCLUSION

This chapter has been focussed on the character of educa-tional gerontology and several of the issues within it. Knowledge of the elements of this cross-disciplinary field allows practition-ers to better comprehend the complexities beneath the surface of much educational practice. It is always useful as an educator to be aware of the philosophical underpinnings of educational activities including the reality that we are never neutral agents and should not pretend to be. Assuming an ethical position means that we need to declare our moral position so that older learners can make better educational judgments. For example, if we believe that educational practice should involve a holistic approach in which expressive and instrumental education both have relevance to older adults' lives, we can be alert to programs which distort this balance. By our adopting a more critical stance to educational gerontological practice, we heighten the prospect of fair play and more equitable sharing of educational resources.

CHAPTER 3

Understanding Aging

The quest to understand aging in its fullest sense has been with humanity since time immemorial. The lifespan of humans has not altered but the expectations of people, at least in Western countries, to live at least three score and ten years have been heightened. This increased life expectancy is related to a number of factors, prominent of which is the advent of more advanced health services and technology. Other factors associated with longevity include higher fertility rates during the early 1900s (when most of today's elderly were born) and the changing patterns of immigration as survivors of waves of new immigrants age (Koopman-Boyden, 1993).

Population or demographic aging is not restricted to any one nation (for example, the USA) or type of political system (democratic versus totalitarian state) or cultural configuration (Western versus Asian countries). The world at large is experiencing a significant shift towards increasing numbers of people living longer in Laslett's (1989) third age. It is sobering to consider that in countries with massive populations (e.g. China), a one percent change per year in the proportions of "older people" (however the concept is defined in that context) can result in very large numbers requiring the basics of life (food, shelter, a sense of community). There are huge policy implications at stake when resources in society (including education) may be restricted or when the demands of one sector of the population are pitted against those of another.

The purpose of this chapter is to explore what aging means from a variety of perspectives. Initially, it will address more individualistic explanations of aging (and their limitations), linking these perspectives with some of the adult development literature, including psychological and cognitive approaches. Then the attention will be placed on more social and macro level explanations, with particular reference to sociological theories of aging and the social construction of aging. Finally, these theories will be related to practice and what they should mean for educators.

THEORIES OF AGING

The notion of what "old age" is or might be is historically and culturally defined. Yet the essential questions around aging are not specific to one context—for example, why do we age? What does it mean to be old? Why do some people adjust to aging better than others? Why is the status of "old age" so low in many countries? These questions are asked everywhere with only some resolution in terms of satisfactory answers.

Within the New Zealand context (which parallels most other Western nations), social scientist Koopman-Boyden (1993) has produced a helpful table (Fig. 3.1) of the relationships between a discipline, the commonly associated theories and the types of questions asked about aging.

The table is reproduced here to emphasize the myriad of perspectives that abound in relation to explaining aging.

Biological Explanations

Within the biological domain, there have been a range of theories concerned with answering the questions of "why do we age?" and "why do we eventually die?" Generally, the biological and psychological sciences tend to focus on physiological and psychological aging, the causes of mortality and the relationship between age and functional capacity. An example is *stress theory* which suggests that sudden and unexpected stress over a person's lifetime can result in physical wear and tear. So, those whose lifestyles engender considerable stress are likely to age the fastest. As this commonsense view has not be proven or disproven, it remains as just another hypothesis to be tested.

Discipline	General Theory	Specific theory	Question Posed
Biology		Rate of living	Why do we age?
		Stress	Why do we age?
		Free radical	Why do we age?
		Hayflick phe-nomenon	Why do we age?
		Genetic/error	Why do we age?
Psychology	Cognitive	Cognitive decline	Why do we age?
		Continued po-tential	Why do we age?
	Functionalist	Disengagement	Who adjusts best?
		Activity	Who adjusts best?
		Developmental/ life-cycle	Who adjusts best?
Anthropology	Functionalist	Developmental	Who adjusts best?
		Modernisation	What explains the status of the elderly?
Sociology	Functionalist	Disengagement	Who adjusts best?
		Activity	Who adjusts best?
		Exchange	Who adjusts best?
		Modernisation	What explains the status of the elderly?
		Age stratification	What explains the status and adjustment of the elderly?
		Developmental/ lifecourse	What explains the status and adjustment of the elderly?
	Interpretative	Symbolic inter-actionism	What is the meaning of old age?
		Labelling	What is the meaning of old age?
		Subculture	What is the meaning of old age?
		Social phenome-nology	What is the meaning of old age?
	Marxist	Political economy	What explains the status of the elderly?

Figure 3.1: Theories of Ageing
Source: *New Zealand's Ageing Society: The Implications*, p.15. P. Koopman-Boyden. (C) 1993. Daphne Brasell Associates Press. Reprinted by permission.

In an article which discusses adult development literature focussing on physical aging, Glass (1996) describes a range of decremental body changes in older adults. In terms of *physical* capacities he points to decreases in muscle mass, a 30% decline in the cardiovascular system, bone loss (more a problem for women rather than men), stiffening of the joints and reduced efficiency of thermo-regulation. Within changes to *sensory* capacities, he refers to reduced visual acuity, age-related losses in hearing and a tendency to slowness of behavior, especially related to information-processing and decision-making. With regard to *learning capacity and performance*, Glass explains that sensory memory (very short-term memory) and short-term memory tend to be more affected by aging than longer term. That is, there is minimal forgetting of events held long ago but more of a struggle for older adults to remember more recent happenings. He acknowledges, too, that deficits in learning and memory may be related to a host of noncognitive factors such as motivation, health, expectation of poor performance and education.

As part of this article, he elaborates on the implications of decrements in physiological changes in older adults' learning for educators and the ways educators can thoughtfully address shortcomings in performance. The tone of the article is rather depressing—one almost feels like having a clipboard of probable physical changes to be ticked off in classrooms of older adults. Yes, there is a physical reality of likely decline in the performance of older adults in spheres where speed and agility matter but there is also a corresponding opportunity for positive changes in other domains of life.

Functionalist Explanations

A theoretical perspective which has held a lot of sway in educational gerontology has been the *functionalist* approach (identified as related to psychology, anthropology and sociology in Fig. 3.1). This approach has been used to explain who adjusts best to aging and to old age. Its roots in sociology go back to pioneers such as Emile Durkheim, Talcott Parsons, Robert Merton and others who emphasized that individuals need to adjust to society's norms and perform expected behaviors in that society. The focus is on individual behavior within a prevailing social system, not on social structures and how they may limit people's life chances. In the aging context, functionalist theorists are concerned about how older people can adjust to society's norms, about "successful aging".

Prominent among a functionalist approach to older adulthood is the *disengagement theory* (as opposed to *activity theory*). As the name suggests, this theory promotes the view that it is expected that older people will pull back from social engagement and society will not encourage their participation, so that a reciprocal accord is established. Behind this theory is the unspoken notion that as older adults have diminishing physical (and perhaps mental) capacities and a short time left, then they should make way for more energetic young people, especially in the workforce. However, society needs an active, contributing citizenry, not a passive, dependent group of "older folk". Hence, age discrimination in the workforce and practices of mandatory retirement draw upon this kind of spurious reasoning present in functionalist approaches.

Counterbalancing this disengagement approach, is the opposite view. In activity theory, it is believed that one should "use it or lose it". This approach emphasizes the need for older adults to remain active members of society—if they engage in regular exercise, join community groups and keep themselves mentally alert then they are likely to have a more fulfilled life. Within adult development theory, Havighurst's (1972) explanation of *developmental tasks* is an example of this kind of thinking. These development tasks were those age-related imperatives which he believed older adults should achieve in order to remain positive contributors to society. For instance, he identified the following tasks as necessary prerequisites to a successful aging process:

• Adjusting to decreasing strength and health
• Adjusting to retirement and reduced income

- Adjusting to death of spouse
- Establishing an explicit affiliation with members of one's own age group
- Meeting social and civic responsibilities
- Establishing satisfactory physical living arrangements
  (Havighurst, 1953, cited in Merriam, 1984)

Unfortunately, the passage of time has rendered many of these tasks as redundant—what he considered normative in the 1940s/1950s is no longer valid for many people now. For example, the assumption that people necessarily have a spouse is open to question. In addition, there is considerable social class and gender bias underlying some developmental tasks.

Anthropological Explanations

In an anthropological perspective on older aging, Clark and Anderson (1967, cited in Koopman-Boyden, 1993, p.19) identified five developmental tasks in a more recent time period. Specifically, they noted:

- Recognizing the physical limitations imposed by aging (for example, adjusting to a slight deafness)
- Redefining one's physical and social life space (limiting attendance at birthday parties of grandchildren to every second year)
- Finding alternative resources of need-satisfaction (replacing outdoor vegetable gardening with indoor gardening)
- Reassessing the criteria for evaluating self (maintaining one's self-esteem by establishing an identity as the family story-teller)
- Reintegrating values and life goals (being able to confront the question of 'who am I?' with a personal philosophy of life and being satisfied with it)

The very notion of "developmental tasks" and their validity must now come under scrutiny. We need only look at the diversity of peoples and their lifestyles to challenge norms of behavior, prescribed by society, that they "must" do. Are there any longer, in what some people see as a postmodernist world, any tasks which humans must fulfil in a lifetime? Very few, perhaps none.

ADULT DEVELOPMENT LITERATURE

In the literature on human development, the concentration among social scientists has been primarily upon childhood and adolescent development. Among a minority of theorists there has been keen attention paid to adult growth and change and still fewer have bothered to consider aging among elders as a worthwhile area of investigation, apart from the medical profession (where the focus has been on arresting poor health, as opposed to looking at factors to enhance "successful aging"). Among adult development theorists, where lifespan development has been explored, we can glean some understanding of expected norms for older people from examining the latter stages of explanatory models.

Psychological and Cognitive Approaches

Erik Erikson explored the character of psychosocial tasks that individuals accomplish at different stages of life. Unlike Havighurst, he postulated that each period of life entailed a major issue or dilemma to be resolved. At the latter end of life he described the fundamental issues to be of "generativity" versus "stagnation" and "integrity" versus "despair". By *generativity* he meant that older adults look for ways to contribute to ensuing generations perhaps through volunteering, home tutoring, advising grandchildren on life's quandaries or mentoring others in a workplace. With regard to *integrity*, Erikson pointed to the need for elders to find meaning in their existence, to make meaning of what they have done and are doing in their lives. This is necessarily a social task for we find meaning for ourselves through our interaction with others. Older adults, as for any stage of life, need to reaffirm their identity, their social and psychological well-being.

Other theorists of adult development have focussed on cognitive development. As Tennant (1988, p.77) has pointed out (cited in Merriam & Caffarella, 1999, p.140), Piaget's work, though concentrated on children's cognitive development, did set the scene for more serious enquiry for how adult learners develop intellectually. Tennant summarizes Piaget's salient contributions to this field as:

- The emphasis on qualitative rather than quantitative developmental changes in cognition
- The importance attached to the active role of the person in constructing his or her knowledge
- A conception of mature adult thought (that is, formal operations).

Subsequent studies have explored the validity of formal operations thinking, proposed different stages or looked into how adults solve "real life" personal problems (Merriam & Caffarella, 1999).

Other cognitive theorists have entered the domain recently, including those who have examined women's ways of knowing (see Belenky, Clinchy, Goldberger & Tarule, 1986). Belenky and associates claim that women have distinctive developmental issues to contend with, from a simple position of "silence" to increasingly complex conceptions of knowledge—"received", "subjective", "procedural" and, finally, "constructed knowledge". While these five positions are not readily categorizable as stages of cognitive development, they do point to underlying issues for women of empowerment and the need to relate the construction of knowledge to personal and collective experiences. The upshot of these approaches has been to depict individual variation in cognitive ability as large and that older adults are as likely as anyone to experience differential cognitive processes. In the work of Riegel (1976), tension, contradiction, ambiguity and paradoxes are perceived as common to all human experience, as the basic ingredient in creativity and mature thought. Reminiscent of Marx's dialectic, Riegel provides a more dynamic perspective on mature adults' thinking capabilities, suggestive of life's complexities.

The enquiry undertaken by Labouvie-Vief (1984) focussed on a more contextual perspective to adults' thinking processes. She challenged formal logic as the apex of cognitive development and posited that we need to look more closely at a person's social context to account for changes in an older adult's thinking. Chronological age is likely to be less of a marker than a major life event such as retirement or death of a loved one. Or, as Merriam and Caffarella summarize (1999, p.167), "Social, cultural, economic and political forces help shape both how we think and what kind of knowledge we value". These sentiments echo those of sociologists of education who advocate for a more socially contextualized view of human development.

One issue related to cognitive development has been the relationship between intelligence and aging, the prevailing belief being that intelligence undergoes slight decline as one ages. From a psychometric perspective, where rigorous attempts have been made to measure "intelligence" based on performance in tests, this adage has held some validity. This is because, for the most part, it has been speed and agility that have mattered most in the tests. In this instance, it has been *fluid intelligence* that has been accentuated. Merriam and Caffarella (1999), quoting the work of Cattell, describe it as "the ability to perceive complex relations and engage in short-term memory, concept formation, reasoning, and abstraction". In contrast, *crystallized intelligence* is defined as "sets of skills and bits of knowledge that we each learn as part of growing up in any given culture, such as verbal comprehension, vocabulary, and the ability to evaluate experience" (1999, p.175). It is the latter type of intelligence that older adults are believed to retain and continue to build on throughout life whereas fluid intelligence generally declines as early as 35 or 40. More recently, as traditional notions of intelligence have been severely critiqued, other constructs have emerged, such as Gardner's theory of multiple intelligences, which capture a more holistic view of what intelligence(s) might entail. In addition, Goleman (1995) has stressed the importance of *emotional* intelligence, as a counter force to cognitive abilities, as vital for an individual's repertoire of social competencies to successfully engage with life. (For further discussion on intelligence and aging, readers are referred to Merriam and Caffarella, 1999, chapter 8).

Perspectives from Life Transitions Approaches

Some adult development theorists have stressed that throughout life we go through events and transitions in which we have varying levels of control of the outcomes. Some events may be personally time related (e.g. retirement), some may not (e.g. civil war). One distinction over types of life events has been to differentiate between "individual" and "cultural" events. Examples of the former include birth, marriage and death; instances of the latter include major social movements, historical happenings and reactions to natural disasters. Obviously, these individual and cultural life events do intersect to set the platform for a person's unique passage through a lifetime. Transitions, those periods of living which vary in length, but usually connect more stable periods, can involve episodes of significant individual growth. In the case of an older couple, for instance, there may be a transition period from when one partner terminates paid work to when the other does the same.

Pioneers in research on the timing of events in (later) adulthood were Levinson and associates (1978). They were interested in studying periods of stability and change, continuity and discontinuity in people's lives (originally focussed on men's). Their explorations revealed that adults move through a largely predictable sequence of stable and transitional periods that match chronological age. As explained by Merriam and Caffarella (1999, p.102), "components of this changing life structure include marriage and family, occupation, friendships, relationships to politics, religion, ethnicity, and community, and leisure, recreation, and memberships and roles in many social settings".

Although these studies provided some insight into possible adult life patterns, there was not a specific analysis of older adulthood per se.

Fisher (1993), on the other hand, focussed exclusively on later adulthood in an attempt to provide more detailed accounts of developmental periods in this time of life. From this qualitative study of 60 older adults ranging in age from 61 to 94 in which they were interviewed on events and transitions in their lives, he devised five periods for the activities and experiences of older adults. These periods and their characteristics are summarized in Figure 3.2:

Essentially, Fisher's findings of alternating periods of stability (periods 1, 3, and 5) and transition (periods 2 and 4) are congruent with Levinson's. Both transitions for older adults present a dramatic change in lifestyle. The first constitutes a move from a lifestyle of middle age to one of older adulthood; the second entails a move from a state of independence to one of dependence. One of several implications from this study is that there is a continuing need to reappraise the goals and activities of older adults and the kind of education of most use at that time. Practitioners should be constantly aware of the need to undertake on-going needs assessment and readjustment of programs based on reappraisal.

Gail Sheehy's analysis of people's lives in *New Passages* (1995) provides a contemporary view of how change and transitions can impact upon individuals in society. One of her salient observations is that people who now consider themselves as "middle-aged" would have in former times seen themselves as "old". That is, middle-age has moved into an older age group—what Neugarten (1976) calls the "young-old"—so that the norms of behavior for today's baby-boomers are being recreated towards a more "ageless" society, where age is less a signifier of predetermined patterns of behavior.

Perhaps the most significant facet of the life transitions literature has been the way that such occurrences trigger learning, that is, people have used learning to cope with life's crises. In this instance, the life transition is seen as the antecedent to

1. Continuity with Middle Age

Retirement plans pursued
Middle age lifestyle continued
Other activities substituted for work

2. Early Transition

Involuntary transitional events
Voluntary transitional events
End of continuity with middle age

3. Revised Lifestyle

Adaptation to changes of early transition
Stable lifestyle appropriate to older adulthood
Socialisation realized through age-group affiliation

4. Later Transition

Loss of health and mobility
Need for assistance and/or care
Loss of autonomy

5. Final Period

Adaptation to changes of later transition
Stable lifestyle appropriate to level of dependency
Sense of finitude, mortality

Figure 3.2: Characteristics of the Five Periods of Older Adulthood
Source: J. C. Fisher, A Framework for Describing Developmental Change Among Older Adults, *Adult Education Quarterly*, vol.43, no.2, pp.76–89, copyright (c) 1993 by *Adult Education Quarterly.* Reprinted by permission of Sage Publications, Inc.

learning (a divorce in a marriage influences a man to look for a new career who then seeks out educational possibilities). Quite obviously, not all life events will trigger learning, as Blaxter and Tight (1995) alert us. Yet equally, education itself may trigger a life transition. A woman who studies feminist pedagogy may become conscious of the oppression she has suffered in a marriage and leave her partner as a result (Freire, 1984; Mezirow, 1981). Hence, the links between life transitions and learning/education need to be treated cautiously. It may be more accurate to speak of a dialectic operating here between life changes and educational decision making.

One empirical study illustrating the complexity of the above relationship is exemplified in Merriam and Clark's (1991) study on the intersection of love and work and patterns of learning. (Earlier work by Smelser and Erikson, 1980, on themes of work and love in adulthood had set the scene for this later study looking at the connections with learning). In Merriam and Clark's study, they discovered three broad patterns:

1. a "parallel" pattern in which work and love are intertwined;

2. a "steady/fluctuating" pattern wherein one aspect remains steady while the other fluctuates;

3. another pattern of "divergence" where work and love exist independently or oppose one another.

According to these researchers, work and love can function as a basis for learning about ourselves or others. They further observed that learning was more likely to occur when both work and love were in unison. This study has intriguing implications for older adults because often work is being redefined by them or for them—volunteering may still be a powerful motivator in continuing to learn. Equally, given one's position in the life-course, love can be curtailed by death of a spouse or of close relatives. In short, there is a much stronger likelihood that older adults will be significantly affected by probable loss in one or both aspects of love and work. More research in this area will be necessary to provide greater understanding of these interconnections.

Sociocultural Approaches

Another insightful conception of adult development related to older adults is provided by sociocultural theorists. Instead of focussing on internal individual characteristics, these thinkers have concentrated upon the interaction of people with their social and cultural environments. Older adults normally belong to myriad groups and social networks, inclusive of family, which constitute their social world and frame their knowledge of local and worldwide events. Theories within a sociocultural framework better represent the dynamics of this social world and tend to emphasize the social construction of older adults' realities.

As noted by Merriam and Caffarella (1999, p.121), "researchers have been especially interested over the past decade in the socially constructed notions of race, ethnicity, gender and sexual orientation as they relate to adult development". The area of adult development has begun to emphasize more the social dynamics of older adults' lives and the agency of older adults. The synthesis between psychological (more individualistic, internally oriented) and sociological (more societal, social structural) perspectives has emerged in the development of sociocultural theories. (For a fuller discussion on this theme, refer to chapter 6 of Merriam & Caffarella, 1999).

An example of this kind of approach is provided by Wolf (1998) in her description of "gender roles" and, in particular, Gutmann's (1975, 1987) cross cultural research. Gutmann postulates that men and women change in their orientations after the "parental imperative". In late middle-age gender expectations and norms tend to relax when children are no longer present. So, men no longer feel the need to play the role of "achiever" or "aggressor" and are more comfortable with more nurturing roles and enhancing interpersonal development. On the other hand, women are freer to engage in a wider range of behaviors, including those perceived by much of society as "masculine". Women can become more career oriented and assertive in their desire to achieve mastery in work tasks. This perceived reversal in gender roles among older adults after the

empty nest is supported by anecdotal evidence but a more rigorous study would be required before such generalizations could
be validated. For the present, we can speculate that the range of
behaviors open to both men and women in later adulthood become more expansive and there is considerably more freedom to
experiment with alternatives in the postmodern age. A clear rec-
ommendation for practitioners is that in their dealings with
older adults that they suspend their stereotypes of what men and
women can do and promote more opportunities for both genders to assume roles which may be new to them.

Another way in which sociocultural analyses have increased
their sway among adult development theorists is via the life history approach. In this method, social scientists focus on the
intersection of biography, social structure and history (Mills,
1959). In effect, participants in studies of this type are encouraged to "tell their stories" to reveal patterns which can be analyzed beyond the individual as the unit of analysis. In particular,
the tendency in older adult development is to focus on reminiscence where the interviewee relates significant events and interpretation of these events to the researcher in a "life review".
Butler's work (1982) has pointed to the importance of this approach to older adults' achievement of integrity (Erikson, 1978).
Reminiscence is seen as a natural and sometimes therapeutic response from the individual to the life events that have been engaged in. In my visit as an adult educator to the UK in 2001,
I witnessed a troupe of older adults who dramatized history
and what it meant to them and their families and friends. The
London-based group conveyed in this conference showpiece the
power of collective reminiscence in depicting historical events
(and personal events and reactions to events within that context).

SOCIOLOGICAL PERSPECTIVES ON AGING

Referring again to Koopman-Boyden's (1993) typology, the
discipline of sociology provides several different perspectives on

the aging process. Given that sociology is concerned with the social world which people create and the structures and processes of society and their impact on groups, it is not surprising that there are many varying explanations of how society influences older adults' behavior. Sociological approaches also help to illuminate how society fails to operate positively for marginalized groups, including many older adults. The emphasis taken in this book of a critical gerontological approach includes the political economy theory identified by Koopman-Boyden but is not restricted to it. Sociological approaches from age stratification, labeling, subcultural and social phenomenological theories will now be explored.

Age Stratification

Age stratification theory is one of several theories which concentrates on explaining the status (usually low) of "the elderly" in societies. It enables us to explore "the relationship between biological aging, age-based roles and the ways in which successive birth, or age, cohorts are influenced by different historical events" (Koopman-Boyden, 1993, p.21). This theory looks at the characteristics of different cohorts of older adults at different points of history. The cohort of older adults living in California in the early 1900s would be very different from contemporary groups in the same location (leaving aside for the moment the effects of within group variations—such as urban versus rural). Each cohort develops its own idiosyncracies based on the shared life events of the time, including the access of respective groups of elderly to educational opportunity in their youth. The baby-boomers of today are far more likely to be financially secure, fairly well educated than a cohort of older adults from other time eras in the twentieth century (Walker, 1990). The political economy of the times, and accompanying welfare policies, also influence the prospects of individuals to a decent quality of life.

Labeling

Labeling theory is concerned with the way social actions of older adults are described by themselves and by others and the impact on subsequent behavior. In predominantly youth-oriented societies such as the USA, to be "old" is to be deviant, to stand outside prevailing norms and expectations. Once a person becomes labeled as "old" (perhaps through having just retired from full-time work), then there is an inclination for that person to behave according to stereotypes associated with "old age" for that society. Koopman-Boyden (1993) points to elderly people becoming stigmatized through the use of terms which emphasize their "thing-status" rather than their identity with other people. For instance, expressions such as "the elderly", "geriatrics" or "forgetful" tend to project unpalatable labels on them and help to prescribe their behavior.

A counterargument is that older adults do not have to act out these stereotypical behaviors. They do have freedom of choice. While this is true to varying degrees for individuals, the ways in which society describes older people, as in the media, do provide parameters for behavior which some people may feel obliged to stay within. Often, as writers about deviance tell us (e.g. Becker, 1963; Denzin, 1988), the description tells us as much about the labeler as it does the labeled. When a young adult calls his father "old man" (as my son has on some occasions), this may indicate that he has a limited view of aging and what constitutes "old age" and what "old men" should look and behave like. It can also indicate that both parties recognize the ridiculous nature of the term and use the occasion as a chance to indulge in good humor.

Subcultural Explanations

Subcultural theory entails a group of people sharing some common norms and values and agreeing to behave according to these shared understandings. This applies equally to older adults as it does to adolescents, to a "Learning in Retirement" group as it does to a skateboarding club. In the case of older adults, (self) segregation usually accelerates the development of distinctive characteristics for older people. The location of a retirement village away from mainstream society means that it is more difficult for older adults in this environment to interact with others. A subculture of "village life" can readily become habitual and present challenges for the inhabitants to maintain a balanced view of the external world. The development of subcultures can have ambivalent outcomes—a strong subcultural affiliation may strengthen individuals' sense of belonging and commitment while simultaneously restricting valuable contact with people unlike themselves. In the adult education context, this dilemma also exists for program developers—does one promote learning opportunities which stress the worldview of older adults (their similarities) or does one deliberately engender an age-less society through non discrimination programming practices?

Social Phenomenology

Social phenomenological perspectives on aging are concerned with describing how an old person's reality is understood by them and by others (Berger & Berger, 1976). This perspective often examines "taken-for-granted" views of reality and exposes the underlying assumptions of behavior. It is also concerned about multiple views of reality and how different people in the same situation may interpret events quite differently. For instance, in a hospital caring for older people, the interpretation of that reality by the carer or nurse is likely to be divergent from that of the cared-for person. The notion of an "ideal patient" might be one who is cheerful, accepting, passive and appreciative. Carers may modify their behaviors according to the adherence of the patient to the commonly accepted view of a good patient. A social phenomenological approach would encourage us to get inside the minds of the main players and retrieve and make explicit their in-built assumptions of the situation. The clear implication from this approach is for those working with older adults to not assume too much, to gain the older adult's perspectives on the situation and to minimize negative preconceptions.

CONCLUSION

The focus in this chapter has been on explaining what aging means in the contemporary context. Many different theories try to explicate the intricacies of different facets of this process which every human faces who is fortunate enough to live through to "older age". In each culture, notions of aging and who are "old" and what older people can and should do vary considerably. Even within cultures, depending on one's location in the political economy (related to social class, ethnicity, gender and other factors), there are divergent views on what it means to be "old".

The approach taken here has been to delineate more specific theoretical orientations—such as biological, psychological and sociological—which individually explain some aspects of aging. Taken from a more holistic perspective, the various theories, while often accentuating different elements of the aging process, do provide a more integrated conception of this complex process, despite their points of tension and contradiction. Quite clearly, aging is at the same time a physiological, social and cultural phenomenon, being both time and place bound. The accent of this chapter has been to emphasize more the social and cultural dimensions of aging in the knowledge that other writers have adequately dealt with physical and medical aspects.

CHAPTER 4

Aging and Social Change

Social change has always been with humankind and it has become commonplace for people of any generation to assert that social change has been greatest in their age. Given the predominance of modern communications through most of the world today, the effects of globalization are felt nearly everywhere. The ubiquitous McDonald's signs in urban landscapes and the growing invasion of cellular phones in public places are testimony to how technological change has accelerated in the last two decades. Toffler's *The Third Wave* is certainly upon us as we grapple with advances in how we can communicate with one another in a context of almost immediate gratification of a need (1980). Most Western governments are now enthusiastic about embracing the notion of "lifelong learning" in "a learning society" where education can contribute towards a knowledge economy in a period of rapid social change. But where are older adults situated in this ever-changing world? This chapter seeks to address the social context of older adults in Western societies and aspects of social change. It discusses prevalent images of older adults, including myths and realities concerning them, the role of the state, issues of "retirement", the differential experiences of older age for men and women, and implications for practitioners dealing with elders.

INTRODUCTION

One of the key characteristics of older adults as a collective is their heterogeneity. It would be foolhardy of anyone to project stereotypical images of older adults with respect to how they handle social change. We would expect the usual range of human reactions to any new societal developments, from tight conservatism to extreme liberalism but historical time and cohort effects are likely to be deeply influential in how individuals welcome or retreat from social change. By *historical time* I refer to the actual time in history in which a person lives and the events that individual is likely to have experienced. For instance, the historical period of my father was one in which he had experienced "the Great Depression" and he subsequently spoke often of the impact this had on his outlook on life. One impact was for him to not take risks in life and to be cautious in his work.

The *cohort effect* is also a likely significant factor in one's decision-making and life chances. This refers to a group of people who share the same norms and have similar life experiences. In its broadest context, the "baby-boomers" constitute a major cohort whose life experiences and expectations are quite different from previous generations. As Sheehy (1995) has pointed out in *New Passages*, this cohort is forging new directions for what older people may be capable of, towards the creation of an "ageless" society.

In the context of New Zealand society, a cohort of Maori (indigenous) families migrated from rural locations to the big cities for work during the 1960s and 1970s. This urbanization had a major impact on subsequent Maori settlement and work patterns, especially as communities from rural areas commonly became fragmented in the city environment. Today, while some older Maori return to their *marae* (community meeting place, including formal meeting house and communal facilities) to be with their *hapu* (subtribe) to reinforce their identity, many stay in the urban location. Hence, older Maori have differential experiences in later adulthood, depending to a large degree on the extent to which they adhere to traditional values and gender-associated behaviors.

AGING SOCIETIES

As part of international concern over how to provide for the diverse needs of increasing numbers of older adults, Governments have attempted to put in place social policies which will continue to guarantee older adults a decent standard of living (Borowski, Encel & Ozanne, 1997; Phillipson, 1998). Whenever "concerns" are expressed about the degree to which nations can sustain pensions or superannuation for older adults, there is a perception that younger generations will need to carry a "burden" for the current elderly. Societies have a "demographic time bomb" ready to explode if the economic and social needs of older people are either ignored or given too much credence (Estes, 1991).

The development of social policy with and for older adults is an urgent need in most countries. However, there needs to be less "moral panic" about the perceived burden of "the elderly" and more thorough research on the relative economic situations of older adults as a collective before social policy is enacted which might damage relationships across generations. Caution in this area of reconstructing old age is expressed by Phillipson (1998, p.124):

> We need . . . an approach that can give legitimacy to the variety of experiences which people are likely to have in the second half of life. The crisis of ageing at the present time is that there appears to be no social mechanism for recognizing the range of contributions made by people over the whole of the life course— 'Older people' are now faced with a crisis of invisibility urgently demanding a response both from themselves as well as from political and cultural institutions.

While each country has its own ways of balancing out the respective expectations of the state, employers and individuals in order to maintain older adults' financial security, Phillipson suggests that in Britain the issue of restoring the state pension for the poorest in society "is as much an issue about the kind of old age we want to develop as a straightforward financial issue" (1998, p.128). He argues that reductions in the level of state pensions to a derisory amount conveys a message about society's lack of commitment to older people. Pensions have become a hot topic of debate based on sectional rather than societal-wide interests. He argues that we need to place the allocation of pensions as one for all generations as a collective responsibility.

POPULAR IMAGES OF OLDER ADULTS

The positive image of older adulthood promoted by Peter Laslett (1989) in *A Fresh Map of Life* is still a minority view. His view is one of emancipation from the chains of the past as older adults aspire for self-actualization. However, it is more the reality that the language around the lives of older people is too often reduced to convenient, largely disparaging, descriptors entailing deficit perspectives of this phase of the life course. The history of old age is captured in books such as *Ageing and Popular Culture* and it is often one of invisibility. With respect to the ancient world:

> Older people show up in the record only when they are a problem, and with average life expectancies scarcely reaching mid-adulthood, they were generally too scarce to be more than a curiosity (Blaikie, 1999, p.29)

More contemporary views of older people contain considerable ambivalence—whether they are a "burden" or an "asset" to society is frequently related to the state of the economy. In times of financial stringency, older folk are more often treated as outcasts whose frailties are not required in the workforce; on the other hand, in times of economic largesse, there is plenty of room for older people to contribute to the economy in part-time or full-time work and they are seen as a positive force, providing valuable role models for younger workers (Phillipson, 1998).

In his discussion on the plight of older adults, Blaikie (1999, p.55) tellingly summarizes their situation as follows:

> The roles and statuses of older people in the family, employment, and civil society more generally have been multifaceted. The values placed on these have fluctuated according to political processes which have accentuated economic priorities and thus acted to marginalise older people into a position of structured dependency. Nevertheless, such age differentiation has not gone unchallenged, and it would be wrong to regard chronological age as necessarily disempowering.

In another insightful analysis of the inter-relationships between older adults and social change, the work of Riley and

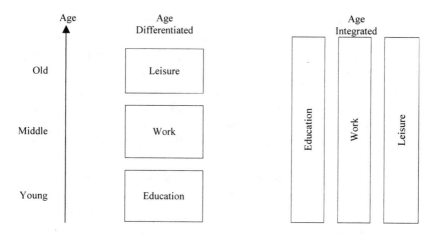

Figure 4.1: Ideal Types of Social Structures
Source: Riley M. & Riley M. Structural Lag: Past and Future. Chapter 1, p.26
M. W., Kahn, R. L. & Foner, A. (Eds.), *Age and Structural Lag.* (C) 1994. Reprinted by permission of John Wiley & Sons, Inc.

Riley (1994) on the concept of *structural lag* plays a prominent role. The problem of structural lag is described as a "mismatch or imbalance between the transformation of the aging process from birth to death and the role opportunities, or places in the social structure, that could foster and reward people at the various stages of their lives" (p.16). In essence, age structures lag behind changes in people's lives. Social structures, norms, and institutions have failed to keep pace with what people actually do in their lives. There is a dialectic in operation here—people are influenced by, and at the same time are influencing, structures in the family, the school, the workplace and the community.

In the figure presented above, the age-differentiated structures on the left divide societal roles and their occupants into three rigid "boxes": educational roles for young people; work roles for the middle-aged (whether paid or unpaid); retirement and leisure for older people. While these structures may now seem outdated, nevertheless this schema has provided the predominant structure and cultural norms for Western societies. It is one which sees education and learning restricted to early in life; one which privileges middle-aged men as the primary breadwinners; one which romanticizes older age (for those lucky enough to get there) as the domain for leisure and recreation.

On the right of the figure is depicted an alternative, albeit, ideal-typical age integration of education, work and leisure as simultaneous activities throughout life. Such a social arrangement would give no stage of life special privilege to learning, work or recreation; it would provide flexibility in lifestyle which some people are already living. For older adults, this model encourages them to continue to engage in learning, whether for instrumental or expressive needs (Glendenning, 2000); it allows for work to supplement whatever pension they may have. This new conception of reality frees up the range of activities available to anyone at any point of life. Obviously, some people because of socially constructed constraints in their lives, are not able to take advantage of a more integrated lifestyle. A 32-year-old woman, unless she tries to emulate superwoman, is going to find that the demands of qualification-seeking and work (in both office and home) may make leisure more of a fantasy than a reality. A 70-year-old man is unlikely to find paid work easy to secure and may be disenfranchised from further formal learning opportunities (Findsen, 2001).

There are potential dangers as pointed out by Riley and Riley (1994)—if flexibility of age criteria for work was pushed too far then abuses could occur such as the well-known cases of children or older people being exploited for their labor. (In this schema, there are obvious connections with the notion of lifelong learning—people are encouraged to continue learning throughout life to keep themselves active mentally, culturally and financially). Professionals working with older adults should be mindful of the emerging age-integrated paradigm and encourage older adults to adopt more diversified roles of worker, learner and recreator.

MYTHS AND REALITIES
OF OLDER ADULTS

One of the effects of using a label such as "older adults" is to suggest that there is a recognizable group of people who share common characteristics. At a simplistic level, this may be true. It is possible to define older adulthood by chronological age alone based on biological aging. Yet, older adulthood is as much a social construction as it is a physiological one (Phillipson, 1998). As a consequence, there are myths which have been built around purported capabilities of older adults and societies' expectations for what they can and should do. In this section, I explore several myths around older adults and the consequences of their continuance.

The Myth of Homogeneity

Older adults are not a uniform group. In fact, there are major variations among subgroups of older adults according to gender, social class, ethnicity and other variables. Arguably, as people age, there are more rather than fewer distinctions among individuals and subgroups (Heppner, 1996). Hence, it is more accurate to speak of the heterogeneity of older adults and it may be misleading to continue to use the label "older adult" without qualification of its usage. There is an inherent philosophical paradox here—on the one hand, the labeling of older adults can accentuate the "otherness" of this large class of people and perhaps unintentionally reinforce their separateness and difference from the rest of humanity; on the other, not to do so renders older adults invisible and therefore, impotent as a political force in societies. No arguments of equality of access to educational resources could be made without emphasizing difference or their special character as a group. Hence, there are times when it is expedient to emphasize the reality of the heterogeneity of older adults; there are also times when some commonality of identity is in their best interests as a collective.

The Myth of Decrepitude

An over-riding image of older adults gleaned from early literature, especially of a medical type, is that of people in declining health waiting around for death (James, 1990; Merriam &

Caffarella, 1999). In the USA especially, much research, especially that connected to cognitive and physiological functioning, has depicted older adults as mentally less capable, as physically frail and as dependent on others for life's necessities. Fortunately, many of the results of this early research have been debunked and the current attitude towards older adults' development is more positive (Drewery, 1991). The vast majority of older adults are fit and healthy, wanting to participate more fully in daily life and wanting to take more control over their own learning. One salient example of this change in orientation towards older adults has been in the area of understanding "intelligence". As pointed out by Merriam and Caffarella (1999), new ideas in intellectual functioning have included a more holistic conception of human intelligence related to the real lives of adults; a greater understanding is developing of the internal and external factors that can strengthen intellectual abilities. Important, too, the emphasis for older adults, as discussed in chapter 2, on *crystallised intelligence* ("normally associated with enculturated information") rather than *fluid intelligence* ("the ability to perceive complex relations and engage in short-term memory, concept formation reasoning, abstraction") has meant that older people can more readily demonstrate "intelligence" accrued over a longer period of time—what might be thought of as "wisdom" in some cultures (Merriam & Caffarella, 1999, p.175).

The Myth of (In)Dependence

One of the strongest beliefs promulgated in adult learning literature is that adults have the capacity to be increasingly independent as life continues (Knowles, 1980). The notion of *self-directed learning* has been attached to this ideal of the independent person (usually male). Indeed, American adult learning theorists such as Mezirow (1981) and Brookfield (1986) have depicted the independent learner as the epitomy of progress. However, the adult learner does not exist in a social vacuum but is linked to other people in social relationships. Nobody can be fully independent, except perhaps as a hermit.

A common perception of older adults is that as they enter the upper limits of the third age, they become increasingly dependent on others, often close family. Death is inevitable for everyone so sooner or later each of us can become more dependent on others for basic needs. This is a physical reality not to be discounted. However, as Drewery (1991) argues, it is much more helpful to emphasize the notion of *interdependence* in adulthood. Each person has knowledge and skills not readily replicated by others (each of us is unique); these are often exchanged in daily life for things we need. For example, Fingeret (1983), in studies based in a so-called "illiterate community", noted that adults exchanged goods and services with one another to enhance the quality of their lives. Older adults do similarly with those from younger generations. Grandparents and grandchildren take part informally in intergenerational knowledge and skill exchanges. Sometimes these kinds of exchanges are institutionalized in educational programs (Lamdin & Fugate, 1997). In summary, there is considerable interdependence amid older adults which affects their learning patterns.

The Myth of Consumer

Frequently older adults have been depicted as "takers" in society, of receiving financial payment from governments (at least in Western countries) while producing little in return. (Of course, older people have been the taxpayers of previous generations). Within adult education, this image of consumer has been quite strong as is related to a *needs-based* approach to the education of older adults. McClusky (1974), a pioneer in educational gerontology in the USA, distinguished between different types of educational need, as already discussed in chapter 2: coping needs; expressive needs; contributive needs; and influence needs.

The depiction of older adults as consumers has been strongly associated with educational programs which emphasize coping and expressive needs rather than contributive and influence ones. Elders have been encouraged, by and large, to adapt to the status quo, to the prevailing social system. Courses in "Adjusting to retirement" or "Becoming self-sufficient", for example, focus on such coping skills. Also, expressive forms of adult education tend to reinforce individualistic pursuits, to encourage the person towards self-improvement rather than to community development. These two categories of programs (based on coping and expressive needs) depict older adults as consumers of education, as reactors to what society has to provide. As will be emphasized later in this book, much of the potential for older adults will rely on their participation as *producers*, more particularly based on contributive and influence needs.

AGEISM AND DISCRIMINATION

For people who have been made redundant in mid-life, the reality of finding new meaningful employment can be frightening. In particular, if a person is a member of a marginalized group, it is even more difficult to secure work as such people are often "doubly disadvantaged" (Bourdieu, 1974). In New Zealand, if you are a Maori or Pacific Islander, according to Thomson (1999), you are much less likely to re-enter the mainstream of the workforce. Of course, aside from employment, discrimination—the act of willfully excluding a person from a service based on gender, ethnicity, social class or age—for older people is frequently experienced in health, housing and other social service industries (Bytheway, 1995).

As will be more fully argued in chapters 5 and 6, discrimination also occurs in the education context. Discrimination occurs when providers fail to consider the learning needs of older adults or when institutional practices do not give this group in society an equal opportunity to participate. For instance, physical amenities which require people to climb several floors of a building or are poorly lit make it more difficult for older adults to gain access to the educational situation and ultimately to persevere in their studies. Transport systems which are not attuned to older persons' physical necessities also mean that less able and confident people will not try to enroll in formal classes.

A POLITICAL ECONOMY APPROACH

Within critical educational gerontology, the political economy approach provides a useful framework from which to better understand the social and historical contexts of older adults' lives. In this perspective, older adults' access to education is couched in the social fabric and material conditions of their lives rather than viewed as an individualistic decision made in isolation from social context. From this perspective, the state is an important instrument in regulating people's lives, primarily in the economic sphere, but also in political, cultural and social domains. The state can be viewed as a mediator between the individual and society, endeavoring to readdress social inequalities and disparities in wealth. Further, educational institutions themselves, as instruments of the Government, are not exempt from political and ideological forces that may influence older adults' engagement with them. Hence, in this book, (non) participation in education among older adults is largely viewed from a macro perspective related to cultural patterns and social dynamics in the surrounding society.

This approach is encapsulated by Estes (1991, p.19) as follows:

> The central challenge of the political economy of aging is to understand the character and significance of variations in the treatment of the aged and to relate them to broader societal trends.

In this way it is possible to understand the meaning and experience of old age from an analysis of the distribution of resources in society which in turn are directed by economic, political and sociocultural forces. In addition, social policy for the aged (or more general social policy which has an impact on older adults) is also inextricably linked to these same material and ideological arrangements. Access and participation are examined not from the viewpoint of an individualistic decision-making process but from a sociological context of embedding individual actions in the fuller political and social environment.

The effects of these changes have been significant, especially on those sub-populations who have been marginalized such as African American and Latino peoples in North America, and Maori and Pacific nations people in New Zealand, workers, and many women. Included in this list should be those older adults who are beneficiaries and/or have minimal levels of income to sustain a "reasonable" quality of life. The gaps between rich and poor in many Western countries have widened and the social welfare and health systems after numerous restructurings (Kelsey, 1999) are more fragile than they used to be.

The Role of the State

Why bother with trying to understand the role of the state and its relationship to "old age"? Three reasons are offered by Estes (1998, p20). The state has the power:

1) to allocate and distribute scarce resources;

2) to mediate between the different segments and classes of society;

3) to ameloriate conditions that threaten the social order.

At different periods of time and in varying political-economic contexts, the state has intervened (or chosen not to intervene). For instance, the institutionalization of retirement has been a serious construction of the state. The ability of older adults to continue to work has been linked to the ebb and flow of production relations in capitalist societies. As argued by Phillipson (1998), the experience of mass unemployment was a stimulus for legislative change around retirement in both the USA and Britain. Hence, at a day-to-day level, policy decisions made by the government and its institutions can strongly influence the matrix of choices available to individuals.

Additionally, Phillipson argues that a political economy model provides a solid basis to counter erroneous claims that demographic change is a cause of financial crisis i.e. there is a public perception that the state cannot afford to pay out pensions at particular levels to growing numbers of older adults. This blaming of older people for economic malaise is tantamount to transferring responsibilities from the state to individual older persons. He points out that the class basis of old age policies can actually strengthen inequalities and encourage privatization in areas such as health care and financial support, thus widening the divide between rich and poor.

A political economy approach also enables us to theorize about the relationship between age, race/ethnicity, social class and geographical location. It encourages questions such as "How do different ethnic groups experience older age?" and "How does gender affect the kind of retirement experience older adults can expect?"

Educational Institutions as Part of the State

Institutions of education are part of the state's apparatus in disseminating traditions, values and ideologies (Althusser, 1972). Take, for instance, the higher education sector and its relationship with older adults. Comparatively few older adults frequent formal education and they tend to be primarily from white middle class backgrounds, typically with solid educational credentials. Their involvement tends to be in the arts, humanities and social sciences rather than in more vocational or technical programs; more women than men enter the universities. This trend arguably is to be expected, given the observation that most learning in older adulthood is expressive rather than instrumental (Pearce, 1991).

The institutions of higher education represent a state apparatus in which prevailing ideologies—such as neoliberalism—are promulgated. Ironically, higher education itself has often suffered as a result of these same reforms: there is proportionately decreased spending by the state on education in many countries; increased staff: student ratios have arisen so that teachers deal with larger classes and increased workloads; greater contestability for research funds occurs. In Gramscian terms, universities have tended to develop *traditional* intellectuals rather than *organic* intellectuals (Gramsci, 1971). Traditional intellectuals have tended to emerge from the dominant class(es) in society; organic intellectuals have usually emerged from more marginalized sectors such as working class groups and they continue to advocate for this group rather than become privileged mainstream members of society. The purpose of universities is not so much to criticize the status quo (though in New Zealand universities are permitted by statute to be "the critics and conscience of society") but to acculturate future generations into society's prevailing ways of viewing the world.

In the British context, Stuart (2000), in reviewing the changes in higher education, such as widening participation and the "massification" of the system (trends which are also pertinent to other countries), identifies a crucial sociological "fact":

> Targeting specific groups—who are not participating—seldom implied that the system had to change; rather the implication was that the targeted groups had to change to fit in with the standards of Higher Education (p.25).

Hence, the onus is much more on the "nonparticipating" groups to change their approaches to learning rather than for the institutions of higher education to respond proactively to them. For the older student, higher education appears to be saying "If you want to join us, it will be on our terms". In addition, the reality of the stratification of knowledge between and within higher education institutions in many countries, though seldom as marked as in the UK, nevertheless is a factor which may impact on older adults' preparedness to enter the institution. As a case in point, it is perhaps more comforting for the majority of senior citizens to enter the local community college than to enroll in an elite private university or major public university.

RETIREMENT IN
THE (POST) MODERN WORLD

The structure of the labor forces in most nations is constantly changing, aligned to Governments' desire to have an "up-skilled" workforce capable of competing internationally in the global marketplace. For example, in the New Zealand context, while agricultural products remain the country's major primary export, the services industries (e.g. tourism) have risen in importance. Hence, the nature of work itself is in flux. According to David Thomson (1999), the predominant patterns of full-time paid work, enjoyed without question in the past, are under considerable threat. The notion of a person, more often male, continuing in sustained work until 55 to 65 years of age, is becoming less the norm. Not uncommonly, a person may be prematurely removed from the workforce at age 50 as a result of redundancy, and find it very difficult to resume full-time work. (This may be related to ageism in the marketplace). If a person is a member of a minority group such as Pasifika in New Zealand or a Latino in North America, then the pathway of a career is very precarious indeed. Given that life expectancies are increasing, this leaves many people's lives in considerable uncertainty in the third age. This is a harsher economic reality than the romanticized image of the third age so often projected by humanist third age theorists (Laslett, 1989). In addition, in some countries such as New Zealand, government has curtailed compulsory retirement, thus introducing a new dynamic into the economic landscape. As identified by Phillipson (1998, p.197) "older workers increasingly find themselves on the margins of the labour market—" and their position within it is often contradictory. As the market expands, older workers are encouraged back; if it contracts, they are often first to be forced out.

It is clear that depending on one's position in the labor force, the decision to "retire" may be freely made, forced upon us through redundancy or unfavorable employment policy or made as a reluctant life choice. Some individuals have the *right* to work (employment policies allow this to occur); some (probably most) have the *need* to work. Older adults are treated differentially in both aspects, related to their wider political-economic environments.

The provision of social welfare or mandated private pension schemes in many countries has enabled many older adults to retire when once this was not possible. Also, the promotion of the concept of *active retirement*, spurred by better health amenities, has now encouraged older adults in greater numbers to engage more fully in life, including in achieving their learning goals. The dramatic development of Learning in Retirement (LIR) programs in the USA, Elderhostel internationally, and of the University of the Third Age (U3A) in mainly British Commonwealth countries, is testimony to this phenomenon. Yet for all this positive growth, the reality is that outside of the mainstream middle class clientele of these educational institutions, there are still huge subpopulations of older adults who have been disenfranchised from formal learning opportunities and whose learning patterns we need to know more about.

Given that some people get to retire and some do not (financial need is usually at the root of this decision), it is arguable whether the concept of retirement itself is sustainable. In this age when increasing responsibility for financial security is thrown over to individuals rather than the state, and if neoliberal policies persist, it is more likely that the new life pattern of education-work-leisure identified by Riley and Riley (1994) will continue and become ascendant.

In his recent book *Learning in Later Life* (2001), Peter Jarvis writes of the need to "learn to retire" as well as that of "learning after retirement". He describes retirement as incorporating ritual, especially if there is geographical separation of people—moving home from one state to another—and in terms of social networks. In contemporary secular societies, the ritualistic significance of a "leaving party" from a corporate environment or a "house-warming party" is often lost so that changes in social and work status can remain ambiguous. In addition, the transition from "worker" to "nonworker" may not be so pronounced as many older adults may reduce their paid work commitment in favor of a fractional appointment or choose to undertake unpaid (voluntary) work.

During a period of study leave in the United Kingdom in 1999, I was fortunate to visit and be impressed by the Association for Pre-Retirement Education, an agency with no direct point of comparison in some other countries (e.g. New Zealand). This agency, while engaging occasionally with individuals in helping them to set goals for retirement, was more focussed on working with existing workplaces and assisting companies to more readily prepare employees for retirement. This work is laudable but there is nevertheless the challenge for the vast majority of workers in less caring environments to think constructively about what they will do with their third age. As in any other context for learning, the tendency has been for those people with better than average educational credentials to receive this kind of learning opportunity first (Pearce, 1991).

In terms of learning in retirement, Jarvis identifies the task of learning a new identity as primary. For some, this change in identity may be minimal—the person continues with many of the same work patterns as previously and does not move away from the local area. For others, the identity change is dramatic—a professional person one day; a person of (enforced) leisure the next. In this latter instance, the importance of setting realistic but challenging goals is high in order to avoid disillusionment. For many women, particularly those for whom domesticity has been the prevailing norm, the change of identity is virtually nonexistent and the possibility of a male partner more often under foot can be threatening and anxiety provoking. Whatever the situation, older adults do not have to adopt predominant work and life patterns. In sociological terms, they have considerable *agency* and their identities are not necessarily predetermined by prevailing social norms or stereotyping.

With regard to learning modes in retirement, three common patterns are identified by Jarvis (2001):

1. *The sages*—these older adults are on a continuing intellectual quest and take opportunities to engage in adult learning wherever it may be available—adult education agencies; universities, further education colleges or the Open University. The U3A movement is an example of the kind of environment which would encourage this mode of learner in older adulthood.

2. *The doers*—these are people who tend to focus on skill development in a range of environments such as gardening, arts and church participation, sports and travel. Those who will-

ingly continue work patterns are also included in this category.

3. *Harmony seekers*—these people tend to limit the amount of learning and often avoid new learning opportunities which may not be in accord with their current view of themselves. They are older adults seeking Erikson's "integrity" in their lives, to find harmony with their world.

This typology reinforces the point that there are very divergent pathways which older adults may take, consistent with their developing self-identities.

GENDER AND AGING

One of the truisms concerning the social construction of aging is that gender heavily influences what we experience and how we interpret our world. Women and men experience the world differentially and more typically than not women are disadvantaged by patriarchal institutions in society (Bonita, 1993). The education system is one such social institution where women predominate in terms of numbers of students but are fewer proportionately in positions of responsibility in academia. With regard to older people, the number of women in comparison to men increases as age increases so that late older adulthood has become remarkably feminized. The burden of care has typically fallen on women who now must find someone or the state to care for them (Arber & Ginn, 1995).

Ingrisch (1995), from a qualitative study of 30 women in Austria, describes the contradictions between women's prescribed roles and the reality of their daily lives. The study focussed on the socially transmitted images of women's roles and how these roles were related to age and identity; it also took into account the historical context in which the women lived. From the interviews, two levels of experience were apparent. At one level some women conformed to society's expectations as they did "the right thing". Another level dealt with the women's suppressed wishes and longings. The contradictions and tensions emergent from the study demonstrated how the women sought a balance between the outer (public) and inner (private) worlds. For example, while some women adopted the role of "the good grandmother", others actively resisted this conformity.

In the learning arena, women tend to predominate as "returners" to education as mature-aged students (McGivney, 1996). In most instances, this is inspired by instrumental purposes as they attempt to get back into the workforce but their choice of subjects tends to differ from men's (towards more helping and caring professions). At the time of retirement for many men, some women find themselves as the primary breadwinner (though often in part-time positions). Phillipson (1998) depicts the dynamics around retirement as problematic—retirement has been more stereotypically perceived as a "man's problem" in which he disengages from his major source of identity and status; this situation is not usually shared by women. The (post) modern world renders traditional views of retirement as rather archaic because retirement is currently clearly much more complex a process than it was previously (e.g. increasing demands on grandparents as caregivers when both parents work). In this situation, where the concept of retirement has become so slippery, the issues around preretirement education become much more challenging. For instance, what is its essential purpose and what is the best form of education for such people?

For many women there is a clustering in low-paid jobs with limited or nonexistent pensions. The experiencing of "retirement" may be very different for women whose income and quality of life may be attached to a husband's (Phillipson, 1998). And retirement from what? The vast majority of caring and volunteering work exercised by women is likely to continue, regardless of retirement. In contrast, it is foreseeable that those men who have retired from full-paid work will need to find volunteering work and/or learn more expressive roles as they enter older age or else enter what some have labeled a "roleless" state.

CONCLUSION

In broad terms, this chapter has been concerned with the social and material conditions of older adults' lives which vary considerably according to the political economy context i.e. according to social class, gender, ethnicity and other factors such as geographical location (urban/rural). It has examined some of the myths surrounding the lives of older people and discussed the major social policy area of retirement amid significant social change in most societies. The important issue of the differential treatment of women in older adulthood was addressed because of its increasing feminization.

Quite clearly, there are major implications for the state and educational institutions. The state needs to deal with the issue of equitable distribution of resources to all in society but especially older citizens for whom the prospect of continuing work is distasteful or a distant reality. For the state, there is still a major role to play in the provision of public facilities and social welfare to ensure that different subpopulations of older adults are treated equitably. Educational policy internationally needs to become more attuned to the ongoing learning needs of people throughout life and encourage older adults in particular to pursue formal education opportunities as a right. For education institutions, there is a major challenge to become more relevant to various subgroups of older adults, particularly those peripheral groups, such as unskilled workers and ethnic minority men, who have been alienated from mainstream education provision.

CHAPTER 5

Older Adults and Participation

The question of participation in adult education has been longstanding and has been analyzed by many prominent theorists in this field. Surprisingly, given this plethora of theoretical investigations, empirical studies and policy reports from around the globe, the treatment of older adults per se, has been relatively scant. However, as a marginalized subpopulation, older adults' issues have often been neglected (Blaikie, 1999) so from this perspective of relative invisibility the lack of attention is more comprehensible.

In chapter 2, the wider parameters for understanding learning for older adults were explained. In particular, the threefold distinction between informal, non-formal and formal learning was featured to illustrate that learning occurs throughout life and is life-wide. In addition, the issue of what constitutes "education" was discussed, with special reference to older adults' education and corresponding philosophical underpinnings. Learning for older adults and their participation in education is readily understood from a lifelong learning approach, emphasized in this chapter.

Frequently the issue of (non) participation has been concerned with the engagement of adults in planned educational activity, more often than not, supplied by an agency where formal classes are the norm. In this situation, "participation" is really attendance of older adults in learning events planned by somebody else and provided to the senior citizen as a service. The older adult is a consumer of this service (not a producer). This occurs most strongly when the learning needs of older adults are linked to coping and expressive mechanisms (consis-

tent with a *functionalist* approach to education). From a functionalist perspective the intent of society is to integrate older
adults into the wider population so that social cohesion is main-
tained and they make the required adjustments to be worthwhile
citizens (Glendenning, 2000; Meighan, 1981)

In this chapter, while a conventional approach to older
adults' participation will be discussed (in which adult learning
and participation theory is applied to *older* adults), a wider,
more liberating, notion of "participation" will be introduced.
Older adults are seen to engage in manifold fruitful learning
activities, many of which are self-directed and independent of
an educational provider and others of which are community-
based and nonformal.

AN OVERVIEW OF ADULT PARTICIPATION

Within the realm of participation research, there are at
least two main types:

• studies which draw on psychological models of behavior to
  analyze participation in terms of the individual motivations
  of people to participate or not; and
• sociological analyses which look at participation in terms of
  social groupings and the social functions that the patterns of
  participation reflect (Benseman, 1996, p.296).

In this context of older adults' learning patterns, while
there will be discussion on both types, the focus is on the second
of these general research perspectives.

In sociological terms, adult participation is important because it can be readily demonstrated across diverse national
contexts that the bulk of engagement in structured learning is
undertaken by mainstream society members, not by marginalized groups. In fact, some theorists argue that education is far
from being an equalizer of (older) adults' opportunities but a
reproducer of inequalities extant in society (Bourdieu, 1974;
Collins, 1998; Giroux, 1979). Typically, those who have already
benefited from previous education are more likely to get more

(as unsurprisingly, they have greater knowledge of how the system works for them and they are intent on retaining the status quo). As Tobias (2001) rightly points out, extensive and ongoing survey research in several countries has reinforced the reality of a "great divide" between educational participants and nonparticipants within the adult population.

Internationally, the development of large-scale surveys of adult education participation is relatively recent. The massive study conducted by Johnstone and Rivera in 1965 in the USA heralded further studies, predominantly in America, which provided valuable insight into the richness and diversity of adult learning. While there was widespread criticism of the largely positivist orientations of many surveys (for example, see Rockhill, 1982), they did fulfil the purpose of documenting trends and raising questions for subsequent research. In particular, the divide between participants and nonparticipants, related to socioeconomic status, was confirmed. The study itself, as reported by Merriam and Caffarella (1999), looked into who participates in what. Johnstone and Rivera concluded that 22% of American adults participated in one of the forms of learning i.e. an activity in which the person acquired some type of knowledge, information or skill. The major correlates of participation were found to be age and extent of formal schooling. In the New Zealand context, Benseman (1996) provided a portrait of the types of people who tend to avail themselves of adult and community education programs, derivative of Johnstone and Rivera's 1965 original. The Benseman profile includes disproportionately high numbers of:

- those who have attended school more than an average amount of time and received formal qualifications
- women (although men tend to be a majority in more vocationally oriented courses)
- those under 40 years of age
- Pakeha (European)
- those who have above average incomes
- people who are in full-time work and most often in a white-collar occupation.

Conversely, those who miss out have tended to be the elderly, ethnic minorities, immigrants, those who left school early and those on low incomes—the marginalized. This profile of mainstream society members being the major recipients of more formal adult learning has been validated in other cultural contexts.

Early Studies on Motivation

In terms of motivational orientations of learners, the early qualitative study of Houle described in *The Inquiring Mind* (1961)—in which he delineated orientations as goal, activity or learning—set the scene for more ambitious studies such as Morstain and Smart's (1974) study of 611 adults in New Jersey. These researchers were interested in identifying the major reasons why adults would participate in further education. This six factor analysis provided the following learning orientations as significant for adults:

1. Social relationships

2. External expectations

3. Social welfare

4. Professional advancement

5. Escape/stimulation

6. Cognitive interest.

The application of these factors to older adults would probably reveal a greater connection to 1, 3 and 6 above. However, the world is now more complex than when this study occurred, and given the ongoing need for older people to continue to assert their economic independence in Western style countries, the other three factors cannot be lightly discounted. As people more frequently change their occupations, even into later life, it is not unreasonable to expect that for some older adults profes-

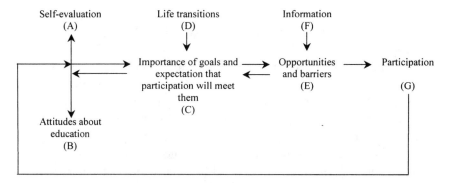

Figure 5.1: Cross's Chain-of-Response Model for Participation in Adult Education
Source: Learning in Adulthood: A Comprehensive Guide, S. B. Merriam & R. S. Caffarella, copyright 1999, Jossey-Bass. Reprinted by permission of John Wiley & Sons, Inc., p. 67.

sional advancement may still be a strong motivator. Practitioners should be aware of the possible multiple motivations of older adults to learn and not assume that usual reasons apply in a specific instance.

Models of participation have been promulgated by leading adult educators in different sources. Readers are invited to look at the second edition of *Learning in Adulthood* (1999) by Merriam and Caffarella to canvass a range of theoretical explanations of adults participation, most of which can be readily applied to older adults' contexts. As a case in point, I have selected Patricia Cross's Chain-of-Response (Fig. 5.1) model for discussion of how older adults might be influenced towards participation.

In this instance, I am presenting the case of a 65-year-old Maori woman who lives in a small town in New Zealand on the east coast of the North Island, about 50 miles from a main city center.

At stage (A), a person engages in self-evaluation. Here a person's self-worth and self-perception influences future decision making. The woman in this case study would need a positive view of herself as a Maori in a predominantly European society; her immediate environment is likely to be in the midst of *whanau* (extended family) who would traditionally give her support.

Stage (B) entails attitudes to education. If her early socialization, including schooling, was not Maori-friendly, the prospect of going further is limited. At varying points of European colonization in New Zealand history, Maori children were actively discouraged from using their own language.

At stage (C)—the importance of goals and whether they are achievable—the woman would be more likely to engage in education if the goal were collectively conceived and she could gain some benefit for her kin. Seldom is education perceived as an individual pursuit in this indigenous society.

Stage (D), in which a life transition can have a powerful impact, could relate to this woman having recently become a grandmother or even great grandmother or to a move back from an urban context to a rural community network. Opportunities are not plentiful in rural villages and barriers can be considerable at stage (E). Transport is nearly always a major concern but willing *mokopuna* (grandchildren) can usually help.

Information—stage F—is more likely to have come through informal channels of whanau than through European style marketing. Participation at stage (G) will also be highly dependent on the perception of culturally relevant knowledge and the appropriateness of the activity to a woman of her age who would normally enjoy high status among kin, especially in a rural context.

Hence, the convergence of many positive features of her life will need to occur for her to have any chance of participation in what is probably to be a practical or skills-based activity— the weaving of some garment where social involvement is high is one such possible learning event.

The point of including the above case study is to illustrate how some generic models of participation can be usefully employed with regard to older people's learning. What such models commonly leave out are the social context and material conditions in which older adults are located and the political environment of which they are part. These factors of the political economy must always be incorporated into any meaningful discussion on educational participation.

Participation in Mainstream Adult Education

Older adults' involvement in *mainstream* adult education has not been commensurate with their percentage of the population. In most Western countries, little hard evidence exists on the extent of older adult participation on a national basis. One international study, the International Adult Literacy Survey (IALS), comparing 12 OECD countries, indicated that in the 56–65 age group (no older age group was surveyed) New Zealand had approximately 25% participation and Australia 18%. It is interesting to quote the New Zealand Ministry of Education's views on older adult performance in the literacy study:

> The relatively poor performance of those in the eldest age group may be related to factors such as the much lower proportion of this cohort receiving post-primary education—for example, 45% of those in the 55–64 years old cohort completed upper secondary education compared with 60% of the 35–44 years old cohort.

Hence, the relative poorer performance is largely attributed to level of previous education, a common explanatory variable. In the immediately following sentence, the report speculates:

> Other possible considerations include the ageing process itself which is known to adversely affect the cognitive functioning of some individuals (1996, no page).

Here the stereotypical factor of cognitive decline is invoked in a clumsy attempt to explain nonparticipation. The Ministry of Education could dare to look at more sociopolitical factors as reasons for this performance level.

It is known from the United Kingdom, though, that participation in formal learning institutions (e.g. universities, local education authorities) is negligible (Walker, 1990); there is no reason to doubt the wider applicability of this remark to other

Western countries. An interesting exception in the British scene has been participation in the Open University (OU) where older adults constituted 4.5% of the total undergraduate population (90% of all older higher education students in Britain) in the mid-1980s. This suggests that it is the mode of distance learning which is the significant factor in their participation; recent popularity of SeniorNet, a network of senior adults engaged in electronic communications, provides additional evidence to support this claim.

In the recent policy document disseminated by the National Institute of Adult Continuing Education (NIACE) in the United Kingdom entitled *Learning to Grow Older and Bolder* (1999), participation of older adults was analyzed and the picture depicted above was confirmed. More specifically, Carlton and Soulsby cite Naomi Sargant et al.'s study, *The Learning Divide*, wherein a population sample of 4,755 older adults were asked about their efforts to consciously choose to learn something, as evidence of older adults' learning patterns. It was found that:

> while more than 2 in 5 of the whole population over the age of 16 were currently learning, or had done so over the previous three years, only 1 in 4 of the 55 to 64 age cohort, 1 in 5 of the 65 to 74, and less than 1 in 7 of people over 75 did so (Carlton & Soulsby, 1999, p.22).

The general observation that "participation in learning declines with age" (ibid) needs to be tempered by knowledge of the type of activity and preferences of older adults for locally accessible learning opportunities.

People outside of this profile (including older adults) are typically marginalized in terms of access to education. For older people, the historical time in which they were children in schools, is more than likely to heavily influence the extent of their "disadvantage". Also, if we analyze the heterogeneity of older adults—look at specific subpopulations within older adults— then we are likely to find that participation is strongly associated with previous educational experience, gender, race/ethnicity and social class (Carlton & Soulsby, 1999). Educators, as practitioners, need to be sensitive to these differentiating variables and how they impact on varying groups of older adults' "connectedness" with varying types of education provision.

A recent study of a Western Sydney University of the Third Age (U3A) group undertaken by Williamson (2000) sought to understand gender issues in older adults' participation in learning. He noted that women outnumber men in this learning-based organization by a ratio of four to one. In speculating on the reasons for this discrepancy, he noted that women tend to outlive men (so there are more to draw upon), women leave employment at an earlier age than men, and there is differential marital status between men and women in the third age (as men who have lost a spouse are more likely to remarry). His case study revealed that gender differences in U3A membership and the relatively low participation rates of men reflect a variety of issues related to retirement.

In examining the gender differences in what men and women do in retirement two main features emerged. Men are inclined to sit and women feel free to undertake things left from their second age. Williamson argues that these patterns have much to do with gender socialization over a lifetime, coupled with their formal education and life experience. These life events have shaped their personal dispositions and outlooks on living in the third age. He alerts readers not to be too hasty in jumping to conclusions about these gender differences revealed in this case study:

> These and other retirement issues need to be investigated further lest new stereotypes emerge which blame men for their apparent lack of interest and mental inactivity and applaud women for their get up and go (Williamson, 2000, p.61).

Further such case studies should reveal more data on differential gender experiences in older adults' participation.

Barriers to Learning for Older Adults

There have been many models developed to explain participation (e.g. Cross, 1981) and typologies to identify barriers to people's participation in learning activities. Darkenwald and

Merriam's (1982, p.137) system of categorizing such barriers has been often cited and will be used here. They describe the barriers as follows:

> *Situational*—these relate to an individual's life context at a particular time i.e. the realities of one's social and physical environment
> *Institutional*—those erected by learning institutions or agencies that exclude or discourage certain groups of learners
> *Informational*—institutional failure to communicate information on learning opportunities
> *Psychosocial* (attitudinal or dispositional)—individually held beliefs, values, attitudes or perceptions that inhibit participation in organized learning activities.

For older adults, all levels of barriers may pertain and for some individuals each category may have relevance in decision-making. Some examples of plausible explanations for each of these factors follow:

> *situational* barriers where disability may prevent people's adequate mobility or the need to use public transport may limit access;
> *institutional* barriers could include non user-friendly en-rollment procedures, high fees, an inappropriate venue or unexciting methods of teaching and learning;
> *informational* barriers may include brochures printed in too small type and crammed formatting or a failure to display brochures in places which older adults frequent;
> *psychosocial* barriers could be a belief in the adage "I'm too old to learn" or older adults' generalizing from pre-vious poor learning episodes to current programs.

Quite obviously, educators can do much to reduce or ne-gate the effects of the above barriers. Some are not within edu-cators' power to change quickly. These types of barriers will require societal level changes in attitudes to older adults, in practices which discriminate against elders, including policies adopted by local and central government. This observation is reinforced by Walker (1990: p.105) in her analysis of participation:

> The larger more intractable issues that form the real barriers, educational and class status, lack of self-esteem and power, require a more radical solution.

In an insightful endeavor to explain why "nonparticipant groups"—those referred to by Benseman (1996) as marginalized —should participate, McGivney (1991, pp.32–33) provides three different types of argument:

1. *Equity and social justice.*

   Subarguments can briefly be summarized as:
   (i) Opportunities should be open to all members of society, not just the privileged.
   (ii) People usually have a greater chance of fulfilling their potential and improving their life chances through education.
   (iii) Previous education disadvantage can be compensated for through positive action.
   (iv) There is a need to end the "negative intergenerational cycle" whereby parents pass on negative perceptions of education and low levels of achievement to children.

2. *Pragmatism/Expediency*

   (i) Changing demographics require educational adjustments. For example, labor shortages caused by dwindling numbers of young people necessitate the training of older adults. Also, growing numbers of older people need fulfilling opportunities to minimize the use of scarce health resources.
   (ii) Access to continuing education is needed to adjust older adults to changing work and lifestyle patterns.

3. *National self-interest*

   (i) In Britain fewer people participating after school means that there is an under-supply of well-educated and trained people to compete internationally.

(ii) Increases in productivity can be gained from invest-
ment in human capital.

(iii) Engaging more people in education saves on welfare
payments.

Some of these arguments are linked to the "domestication"
of older adults, adjusting them to the predominant economic
imperatives of society. Others are based on more traditional
explanations related to equality of educational opportunity.
Whichever rationale we prefer, the belief most strongly espoused
by progressive educators is that both individuals directly and
nations indirectly would appear to benefit from more participation of older adults in education, whether this takes an expressive or instrumental form (Carlton & Soulsby, 1999).

Most practicing adult educators engage with older adults,
few as they may be, in their programs. A significant issue for
educators is the extent to which they tailor their programs to
the interests of older adults. What is or should be the responsibility of educators towards this group of citizens and what kinds
of learning are most appropriate? Assuming there is agreement
on the provision of education to older adults, who should control the learning process and to what ends? At present these
questions largely remain unanswered but strong suggestions are
given in the final chapter of this book.

GETTING BEYOND PARTICIPATION IN
MAINSTREAM EDUCATION

As already pointed out, Tough's (1971; 1979) conception
of participation has been very much broader than most people
have traditionally conceived of it. In most instances, participation in (older) adult education has been conceptualized in terms
of engagement in more formalized learning activity. Tough's work
unlocked the shackles of participation to include a much wider
array of self-planned projects which people from diverse walks
of life could engage in. A learning project constituted "a highly

deliberate effort to gain and retain certain definite knowledge and skill, or to change in some other way" (cited in Merriam & Caffarella, 1999, p.294). Tough's original work has been replicated in many different contexts and includes Hiemstra's (1976) study wherein 214 Nebraskans, 55 or older, were interviewed (with an average age of 68). Several pertinent findings emerged from this research:

- an overall picture was constructed of an active learner, frequently engaged in self-directed learning and not very dependent on traditional sources of information;
- the stereotype of minority, less educated, blue-collar and lower-class people not being involved in learning was shown to be a nonsense.

It is important to note that Hiemstra's finding regarding the marginalized groups' participation relates to disengagement from *education* rather than learning per se. He concluded that "educators must learn to remove their institutional blinders and recognize that self-directed, independent learning is going on— outside of institutional structures" (1976, p.337).

Hiemstra's findings are hardly earth-shattering in the contemporary world. But Tough's and Hiemstra's studies have demonstrated that we need to ask "What counts as participation?" and "Participation in what?" The range of what counts as useful knowledge or education needs considerable expansion to include a myriad of both instrumental and expressive forms of activity, especially in the informal domain of learning. McGivney, in her 1999 study of *Informal Learning in the Community*, has grasped this concept, reminiscent of Tough's earlier studies. She defines *informal learning* in this study to be:

- Learning that takes place outside a dedicated learning environment and which arises from the activities and interests of individuals and groups, but which may not be recognized as learning
- Noncourse-based learning activities provided or facilitated in response to expressed interests and needs of people from a

range of sectors and organizations (health, housing, social services, employment services, education and training services, guidance services)

- Planned and structured learning such as short courses organized in response to identified interests and needs but delivered in flexible and informal ways and in informal community settings. (McGivney, 1999, p.v)

The application to older adults' contexts should be immediate. While McGivney's extensive study did not focus on older adults per se, it did have a strong community development ethos and sought to link informal learning with educational progression (people moving on to more formal study) and learning pathways. As will be argued in ensuing chapters, the informal learning described by McGivney is the predominant mode of learning for older adults. Such learning can occur in community centers, clubs, pubs, shopping centers, voluntary organizations and a host of other settings. It is usually anchored in the community for the community.

CONCLUSION

In this chapter I have attempted to analyze older adults' participation in a broader context than more orthodox approaches. While some of the standard approaches (theories and models) to understanding adult participation are useful—see Cross's Chain of Response model, for instance (see page 69)— they do not portray the realities for specific older adults with sufficient clarity. From around the Western education world, the refrain of "who already has, gets more" does retain its validity both comparing older adults with the total population and *within* groups of older adults. Lamentably, participation by older adults in formal learning is not what it could be but when we look at more casual, informal learning that emanates from their daily lives, this picture changes to a much more favorable one. So if our definition of "participation" is broadened to in-

clude all types of learning—formal, non-formal, informal—
then older adults are much better placed quantitatively.

The heterogeneity of older adults should not be forgotten.
The divisions found in other sectors of society according to gender, race/ethnicity, social class etc. are also true for older adults.
The reality of the older Maori woman in a rural setting is very
different from a white middle-class male living in an urban
situation. Their likelihood of participation based on a social
analysis is unequal. But then we ask, "Participation in what?"
We need more precise data on what different groups of older
adults do in their lives and the resultant learning opportunities
that emerge out of or accompany these lifestyles.

CHAPTER 6

Provision of Older Adult Education

This chapter is concerned with providers of older adult education and the kind of provision they make available. It deals with "education" rather than "learning" since the emphasis is placed on organized structured learning—formal and nonformal learning rather than the informal—though these boundaries are permeable. Again, the concentration is focussed on *older adults*. The provision that is made available solely to older adults by many agencies cannot always be disentangled from more generic provision. The intent of this chapter is to analyze the character of what agencies offer to older adults, particularly in terms of its appropriateness.

In terms of provision of educational opportunities for older adults, the range is enormous and generally mirrors the complexity found in other domains of adult education. Philosophical diversity is suggested by the framework of needs mentioned in chapter 2. Programs can be concerned with individual development and coping skills or focus on recreational and leisure pursuits. Less often they relate to fostering vocational skills (though this might change with the growing need of retired adults to find further income); still less are they concerned with developing critical capacities of elders to challenge the social order.

WHAT DOES OLDER ADULT EDUCATION LOOK LIKE?

Just as the programs available to older adults are diverse in philosophy and what they encompass, the actual providers (agencies) themselves are similarly complex. I now provide some typologies of adult education provision from different contexts as an indication of the kinds of education available to older adults in generic provision. Later I focus on education designed more specifically for older people.

In the Australian context, the Australian Senate Standing Committee on Employment, Education and Training of 1991 sought to map the field of adult and community education. The emergent matrix of providers and types of programs is recorded here in Figure 6.1:

ADULT EDUCATION AND TRAINING: MAJOR AREAS AND PROVIDER SECTORS

	Adult Basic Education	General Interest	Training/ Vocational	Public Education
Formal Education	*****	**	***	*
Govt. Depts. and Agencies	**		***	*****
Community Providers	***	****	**	*
Private Providers		*****	*****	
Enterprises/ Unions/Prof. Assocns.	*		*****	*

Figure 6.1: Matrix of Providers & Programs
Source: Australian Senate Standing Committee on Employment, Education and Training, 1991, p.25

This matrix is provided as an example of a typology which has been developed to try to encapsulate what might be included in the field of adult and community education. By and large, older adults have been stereotyped as engaging in more *expressive* than *instrumental* forms of learning. This stereotype has developed because "in retirement" older adults are meant to have more time to devote to personal development tasks (as opposed to those associated with paid work). In addition, this false classification has been presented alongside another false dichotomy of *nonvocational (liberal)* and *vocational* education. It is no longer useful to describe educational opportunities so narrowly anymore in terms of the purposes they can fulfil in older adults' lives.

In the case of New Zealand, as indeed for other countries too, the professional field of Adult and Community Education (ACE) has its own national organization to represent a wide range of providers and purposes almost exclusively in the nonvocational arena. In *The Fourth Sector* (1996, p.42), Tobias points out the five subfields identified by that Association as part of ACE:

- Adult basic education
- Second chance education opening the way to further formal education, training and/or employment
- Personal development education which enables an individual to live in a family, group or community
- Cultural education which enables a person to participate in the life of their community
- Education to facilitate group and community development.

The point of mentioning this range of provision is to query the extent to which older adults are involved in each area. There are no simple answers. Depending on the social and economic circumstances of individual elders, each category could be relevant. As a case to consider, new immigrants to a country are quite likely to straddle all domains, especially if English is not their first language and they are entering a Commonwealth country or North America. While the need for qualifications among older adults may not be strong, they may still require "second chance" education to up-skill for work or for citizenry tasks and responsibilities.

In general, there are at least four types of adult education organizations in terms of provision for older people:

- those self-help agencies controlled by older adults to meet their own learning needs (e.g. University of the Third Age [USA]);
- those agencies that develop programs explicitly for older adults (e.g. Elderhostel; the Pre-Retirement Association);
- those mainstream providers who develop some courses which might appeal to older adults (e.g. retirement programs run by centers for continuing education);
- those who ignore or neglect older adults (no provision is made for them and no facilities have been established to encourage their participation). (Findsen, 1999b, p.23).

The reality is that in most communities there are few educational agencies that have been established with older adults as the constructors of the knowledge or that have this group as their primary target. This could reflect the relative powerlessness of older adults in youth-orientated cultures (Phillipson, 1998). However, there are certainly many mainstream providers who have provided a token level of support, that is, they establish a few courses which they hope will appeal primarily to older adults (e.g. preparing for retirement). The harsh reality is that there are still more agencies that have neglected older adults' learning needs. There is an immediate challenge here for raising the consciousness of such providers to their responsibilities of working with traditionally marginalized groups, inclusive of older adult subpopulations.

Outside the Education Sector

The above typology assumes that the organization has an *educational* role. The range of educational options reflects the degree to which these agencies are overtly carrying out provision for older adults. Aside from this categorization of educational purpose, there are many organizations which are concerned about the social issues facing older adults (e.g. Age Concern; City Councils; Grey Power; Help the Aged; the Pre-Retirement Association). Although their principal goals and main activities may not be explicitly related to education, it is likely that education is a means by which they would want to fulfil their mission. Education is often a supportive strategy or a subsidiary goal. Whatever the case, there is also great potential on local or national scales to encourage greater collaboration amongst such agencies and to work alongside older adults in the enhancement of quality living. Learning is a close partner to living; social and educational issues can become intertwined so that by addressing older adults' social issues we are often addressing their educational needs too.

The initiative recently taken by the Blair government in the UK, *Better Government for Older People*, is a realization of the need for organizations to work more effectively on a cooperative basis (Carlton & Soulsby, 1999). While more details of this innovative project are provided in chapter 7, suffice to say here that the sponsoring body, the Department for Education and Employment, at least recognized that a coordinated approach to older adults' issues is required to effectively use scarce resources from multiple players in social education. Whatever our contexts as practitioners, if educational and social agencies can cooperate to focus on the material and social conditions of older adults in communities, it is far more likely that the impact will be more positive and enduring.

Inside the Education Sector

Within the educational context, workers in an adult education agency are confronted with some significant challenges. There is a need for agency workers to become much more analytical about their type of provision and who is benefiting most from it. If it can be readily demonstrated that the older participants in the program are not in proportion to their population in the surrounding district, then some of the barriers mentioned in chapter 5 are likely to be preventing their participation. Agency practices—such as modes of promoting or marketing programs, more particularly the language and photographs used—need to be closely examined for cultural, social class or age bias. Perhaps multiple forms of publicity are required and new ways of communicating with disenfranchised people are necessary. Sometimes agencies use an individualistic framework for communication when a more collective approach, based on direct approaches to marginalized groups, would reap better rewards (Thompson, 1980).

It is not uncommon for adult education agencies to fail to incorporate older adults into the manifold processes of program development. For example, what direct input have older adults had in the planning phase? Have the learning needs and interests of the older age group been properly assessed in a nonthreatening manner? Right through the planning, implementation and evaluation phases of programming there are numerous fruitful opportunities for older adults to be involved (Boone, 1985; Caffarella, 2001). Sometimes an agency working in tandem with an older adults' organization (e.g. Age Concern) can stimulate positive outcomes for both parties, including a reduction in bureaucracy and a reduced call on scarce resources.

In the Workplace

So far, the discussion has been channeled towards *non-vocational* education or the world of adult and community education. Yet older adults, in increasing numbers, are either forced to continue paid work in order to survive financially or they opt for part-time work, perhaps in conjunction with voluntary endeavor. The logistics of global capitalism, technological advances and sheer demographics may steer many older people back into a workforce which may (or may not) be prepared for them. Stereotypes abound, based on deficit notions of older workers' capabilities, that people are past a "use-by date" in their 50s! Fortunately, some organizations and employers recognize the merits of a mixed age workforce (such as the mentoring of young/new workers) and acknowledge that very often older workers bring positive attitudes of commitment, reliability and durability to a workplace (Henretta, 1994; Jarvis, 2001).

One obstacle which employers need to confront is the idea that older workers do not need (re)training because they have less time left with the company or they are less capable of learning. This myth of unsuitability for training or further education is exposed in the National Institute of Adult Continuing Education's Discussion paper of 1993 entitled *The Learning Imperative*. In this document NIACE confirm statistically that training declines with age and urges the British Government and employers to take positive action to address this wastage of human talent. They cite Schuller and Bostyn's Carnegie Enquiry into the Third Age (1992) as the basis for the assertion that:

> nine out of ten employees over the age of 50 receive no training at all; and training and education are used most by those with the most extensive initial education (20% of people with higher education qualifications, compared with 3% with no qualifications at all)" (NIACE, 1993, p.23).

Further, this report points to the importance of recognizing prior learning in making provision for older adults and the imperative to marshal the accumulated experience of older workers as trainers and mentors.

The arbitrary divide between nonvocational (expressive) and vocational (instrumental) learning is gradually being eroded. Community-based educators more often see close links with adult basic education and workplace learning in their own work; people in organizational development and HRD see utility in notions of student-centeredness and cooperative enquiry, largely derived from more community education environments. It is no accident that the national body in Australia renamed itself as Adult Learning Australia (ALA) from the Australian Association of Adult and Community Education (AAACE). In New Zealand, a similar debate emerged at the 2002 Annual conference of the National Association in Auckland but no name change occurred. The new age is one where learning is acknowledged as valid, regardless of where it is acquired and the context in which it occurs. For older adults, the distinction between expressive and instrumental learning is now less salient; older adults can be expressive in work contexts (especially in voluntary work) and instrumental in recreational pursuits.

PATTERNS OF OLDER ADULTS' TREATMENT AND EDUCATIONAL RESPONSES

The provision of older adult education is very much related to philosophical presuppositions, as hinted at in chapter 2. In what is now seen as a pioneering vision for the treatment of the aged and for recipients of education, the modal patterns established by Moody (1976) still have direct relevance today (Fig. 6.2). His four models of education, best understood as a historical record of assumptions made about older adults and their subsequent treatment, is summarized here as a useful testimony to (dis)empowerment of older adults.

The isolation and neglect of older adults in modern society can be related to their status as nonentities—Moody calls this *rejection*. He points to social institutions such as the enforced segregation of the nursing home and the retirement communities of the "gold coast" as evidence of this phenomenon. Educationally, it makes little sense from this perspective to spend money on old people who have little productivity left in them.

In the second pattern of *social service*, Moody describes the institutions of the welfare state, with their propensities to do something to somebody as typical. A whole set of professionals and bureaucrats are established to oversee the distribution of social services and the mentality of passivity pervades this process. This pattern corresponds well with the disengagement theory of aging and it promotes segregation. Its educational response is to keep people entertained and busy, usually in recreation and leisure which matches the image of the dependent consumer of education.

In the third pattern of *participation*, the dignity and autonomy of older people are upheld. The push is to encourage

Modal Pattern	Characteristics	Basic Attitude
Rejection	Segregation; mandatory retirement; poverty, neglect; family abandonment	Repression, avoidance
Social Services	Transfer payments (welfare, social security); professional care; senior centers	Social conscience, liberalism
Participation	Second careers (employment or volunteer activity); senior advocacy; autonomy	Social integration, "normalization"
Self-actualization	Individuation, psychological growth, and self-transcendence	Wisdom, ego-integrity

Figure 6.2: Modal Patterns for Treatment of the Aged
Source: Copyright 1976. From Philosophical Presuppositions of Education for Old Age, *Educational Gerontology*, vol. 1, p.2 by H. R. Moody. Reproduced by permission of Taylor & Francis, Inc., http://www.routledge-ny.com

older adults to live as far as possible as part of the mainstream where activity (not disengagement) is the norm. Educationally, older adults may focus on second careers and on finding creative ways in which to participate fully in society. In this scenario, older adults can find new meaning in a different career or via voluntarism. Education programs can encourage older people to undertake advocacy in areas such as employment, social services and health.

Fourth, the pattern of *self-actualization* is emphasized where spiritual and psychological growth is valued. For Moody, there is something uniquely possible in old age that is not possible in any other stage of the life cycle. He advocates contemplation and meditation as ideal occupations directed to resolving Erikson's dilemma of ego-integrity versus despair. For educators, the championing of the humanities and social sciences in such fields as philosophy, religion, psychology and literature would assist older adults to reach this new dimension of meaning.

The progression of Moody's modal patterns echoes the hierarchy implied in McClusky's four program imperatives based on coping, expressive, contributive and influence needs. In the latter sections of both approaches, the emphasis is placed on programs which help adults to find enhanced meaning in their lives, often of a spiritual nature. But importantly, too, the two writers both see as important the fundamental desire of older adults to contribute actively to society and, if necessary, organize collectively for social action to effect change. In many instances, this amounts to older adults standing up for their own rights and asserting their need for on-going recognition by the rest of society (Phillipson, 1998).

EXEMPLARS OF PROVISION OF OLDER ADULT EDUCATION

The University of the Third Age (U3A)

In the provision of educational opportunities for older adults, the internationally based University of the Third Age (U3A) stands out for its responsiveness, autonomy, innovation and resilience. It is showcased here as an organization controlled by older adults which exemplifies many of the characteristics of a quality educational institution lauded in the nonformal learning literature.

Historically, the roots of the U3A movement began in France in 1973 where a strong relationship was established between traditional universities and retired people. Although the kinds of U3A in France have diversified from the original curriculum emphasis on the humanities and the arts, the "French model" still retains close relationships with universities. On the other hand, the "British model" based on a more self-help ethos, does not have the same reliance on a university for its identity (though in some places, this relationship with a university may exist). The first U3A in Britain, established in 1981, adopted an approach where there is no distinction between teachers and taught (Laslett, 1989). This more open system has tended to spread into some Commonwealth countries (such as Australia and New Zealand) where the autonomous approach of each U3A is held onto steadfastly. Autonomy is especially demonstrated in the ownership of curricula (the right to construct one's own program) and pedagogical practices (deciding which methods of learning are appropriate to each U3A).

U3As do follow a constitution (originally laid down in the British context) but rules are kept to a minimum. Costs of involvement are kept very low to encourage maximum participation and quite often (depending on the size of a study group), the learning events are held in a member's house or a local community hall. Generally, at least in the Australasian setting, the size of classes is deliberately restricted to around 15–20. The principle of using the expertise of the group as an educational resource is taken seriously. The "teacher" usually comes from within the group itself and the session is led by an enthusiast (many of whom may have had professional knowledge of a topic from their work context prior to retirement). The curriculum has normally emphasized the liberal arts with the concept of intellectual stimulation or cognitive development undergirding the selection of content. More recently, the curriculum has broadened to include more recreational and leisure pursuits, not without some controversy within the ranks. A significant feature of the U3A approach is that assessment and exams do not rule the minds of participants. Participation is entirely voluntary and learning is not assessed.

I have been fortunate to be an honorary member of the Auckland U3A Network—as a researcher of older adult learning and as a local University representative. The movement in this part of New Zealand has high morale. At each quarterly meeting of the Network it is not unusual to learn of an oversubscribed membership in a given suburb (numbers commonly capped at 150–200) and the establishment of a new group. The cooperation across groups is outstanding and the passion for learning is high.

As a supporter and sometime critic of U3A, Swindell (1997, 1999) has studied this educational movement in Australasia. He points to some challenges for U3A, such as changing immigration patterns, management issues, research (or its lack), internationalization (as opposed to self-absorption on local concerns) and the new communications technology as especially relevant issues in current times (Swindell, 1999).

In a compelling argument about the links between older adult education and health benefits, Swindell (1997) argues greater attention should be given to how education can contribute to healthy individuals and to a society with fewer medical bills. In a section dealing with the hidden worth of the U3A service to the community, Swindell explores "the monetary worth of third agers" (1997, p.481) and the very important contribution made by volunteer tutors to the organization. He concludes that "the annual value of U3A voluntarism in Australasia will almost certainly be worth several million dollars" (ibid, p.483). Hence, as a voluntary self-help agency, U3A has a broader impact than educational worth since it encourages a healthy lifestyle and embodies the notion of empowerment of older adults.

Wearing a sociological hat, it is possible for me to critique this educational movement for its white, middle-class bias. Given the multicultural environment of Auckland city, for example, one would reasonably expect to see at least some Asian faces plus those of Maori and Pasifika peoples. This does not occur. The membership of U3A is also heavily represented by professional and business people who generally have higher levels of educational attainment than the norm. The exclusion of minority groups is obviously not deliberate but the pervading ethos of the institution mirrors the values of the dominant group in society. These minority groups do not have the "cultural capital" to feel comfortable in this environment (Bourdieu, 1974).

Elderhostel

In the North American environment a large compendium of programs is available for older adults with varying levels of engagement and control exercised by the learners themselves. Manheimer (1998) explains that supportive events and benign legislation have enabled older adult education to expand dramatically in the last two or three decades linked to initiatives such as the 1971 White House Conference on Aging, the establishment of the National Council on Aging (NCOA) in 1976 and the National Endowment for the Humanities (NEH). Amid the emergent movements in support of lifelong learning amongst older people is Elderhostel, a fee-driven program begun in 1975 for short-term, college residency programs originally geared for low to middle income older adults (initially over 60 years).

Essentially, Elderhostel is known as a "travel and learn" program combining tourism with education so that "the world is our classroom". It is "a not-for-profit organization dedicated to providing extraordinary learning adventures for people 55 and over" (Elderhostel, 2003). Currently there are nearly 200,000 older adults taking such adventures in more than 90 countries. One of my own abiding memories of working in the Centre for Continuing Education at the University of Auckland in the mid 1990s was addressing visiting USA-based Elderhostelers on the education system in New Zealand. It was always an enjoyable experience because the groups were so eager to learn and well versed in life's exigencies. My personal experience as a teacher squares with the ideals of the organization which endeavors to "open minds and enrich lives". The "sharing of new ideas, challenges, and experiences is rewarding in every season of life" (ibid, 2003). According to Elderhostel, their programs all share four unique attributes:

- Educational excellence
- Comfortable accommodations and delicious meals
- Extraordinary value
- The warm camaraderie of fellow Elderhostelers.

This claim is compatible with the reasons why adults engage in educational activity (see earlier commentary on adults' motivations to learn in chapter 5).

In a qualitative study exploring how older adults make choices about non-formal educational experiences (in this case,

Elderhostel), Arsenault, Anderson and Swedburg (1998) catego-
rized the 154 Canadian participants as activity-oriented, the
geographical guru, the experimenter, the adventurer, the content-
committed and the opportunist. This research testifies to the
diverse orientations of Elderhostelers to their learning in a travel
context.

As for U3A, the majority of the participants in Elderhostel,
at least in the international side of the operation, emerge from
fairly wealthy backgrounds and successful careers. Elderhostel
is quite typical, according to Manheimer (1998), of the increasing user-pays programs for older adults under the privatization
of education. Participation in Elderhostel is more slanted towards benefiting the individual through intellectual and personal enhancement and is closer to the expressive form of learning, more prevalent among older adults. It is attuned to meeting
individuals' needs and is consumer-driven.

Institutes for Learning in Retirement (ILRs)

The nearest equivalent to the participant-based U3A of the
Commonwealth countries in the USA and Canada appears to be
the institutes (or centers) for learning in retirement. Started as
a peer learning program at the New School for Social Research
in New York in 1962, the first ILR was the Institute for Retired
Professionals (IRP).

As for the "French model" of U3A, the IRLs have traditionally been under the mantle of colleges and universities, particularly centers for continuing education. They offer noncredit
academic programs to which there is open membership. As a result of their typical location within the academy, they have lived
an ambiguous existence at the margins of these institutions—
often using less desirable office and classroom space; little input into the workings of the university; minimal contact with
undergraduate students. Further, they are expected to be self-
supporting and effectively run their own affairs (Manheimer,
1998).

Under the wings of the Elderhostel Institute Network (EIN) which began in 1988, the IRLs have expanded considerably throughout North America, with more than 400 courses available each term (Elderhostel, 2003). Customarily in an IRL, there would be 200–300 members who provide volunteer services in leading programs and serving on various committees.

In a study based at the McGill Institute for Learning in Retirement in Montreal, Clark et al. (1997) investigated the value of peer learning in this type of institution. The researchers' interests were mainly focused on the role of the moderators or group leaders in facilitating the learning of others. They found that "peer learning is student-directed, planned by the learners themselves, and undertaken to suit their personal circumstances" (p.761). While the role of the moderator varied (three related roles of animator, teacher and organizer were identified), their impact was considerable in enhancing the learning of others. For the participants "learning from the knowledge and experience of others, and participating in well-informed discussion, are valued above all else" (p.751). Hence, again, in this institution of older adult learning, the salient features consist of self-directedness, collaboration, student ownership and intellectual curiosity (Houle's inquiring mind).

Within the North American context, there are many other examples of educational institutions established by older adults themselves either under the protection of a public agency or operating independently where the character of the learning is more shaped by the participants.

ISSUES FACED BY PROVIDERS

The relative success of the U3A movement to promote the construction of knowledge of older adults for themselves has been more readily achievable through an independent organization. Further, it is an institution where education purpose is paramount and not subsidiary to any other function. It is easier to be innovative and responsive to learners' needs when the

organization has considerable autonomy and a minimal bureaucracy. Quite obviously, a precondition of fuller autonomy
is independence.

Other providers have less than ideal conditions. When organizations do not have sufficient autonomy to exercise responsiveness to older adults' learning needs, their programs are less
likely to be immediately relevant. The curriculum ideally should
be developed in conjunction with the people who constitute the
principal learners (Caffarella, 2001), as in most IRLs.

In addition, sources of funding can present difficulties as
sometimes finance comes with strings attached. Where educational agencies have relative autonomy, it is sometimes possible
to cross-subsidize programs with a social/cultural orientation
by ones which are readily self-sufficient and likely to produce
considerable profit. In this instance, it is important that man-
agers have a social vision which encompasses nontraditional
groups' needs (a category which includes significant numbers of
elders).

The staffing of agencies is crucial in terms of developing
meaningful relationships with groups of older people. Not only
do they need professional development concerning the realities of older adults in the community but they also require an
attitude to be nonpatronizing and empathetic to their concerns. Having a wide cross-section of age groups employed in
an agency can also assist in recruiting older adults. In participant-
driven organizations such as the U3A and Institutes for Learning in Retirement, staffing is reliant on the capabilities of the
volunteers, so not surprisingly, the quality of service can vary.

Another lesson well learned from self-help older adult agencies is that education is as much about *process* as it is about
product. It is also a collective endeavor as well as an individual
enterprise. Agencies need to understand the significance of developing longer-term relationships with groups of older adults
consistent with the sociocultural context of the learners. The
tendency under a market liberal approach to education is to see
adults as numbers in a room or statistics on a chart from a competitive perspective. This distracts attention away from the fundamental notion that effective teaching and learning occurs in

a nonthreatening supportive situation where social relationships are important and take time to foster (Knowles et al., 1984; Ramsden, 1992).

CONCLUSION

In this chapter I have discussed the character of adult education providers and what it is that they produce in terms of programming. The provision of education for and with older adults mirrors the trends in the field of adult and community education more generally. There needs to be a considered balance between expressive and instrumental forms of educational provision.

Education seldom is delivered neatly parceled for older adults' consumption. Indeed, apart from a handful of organizations whose primary target is older adults such as Elderhostel and Learning-in-Retirement programs, the bulk of providers offer a scant resource for this important group of learners in society. The situation is compounded by the fact that education is also provided by organizations which do not see themselves as "educational" and in which this objective is relegated to a minor function.

An unfortunate reality, according to pioneer Moody (1976), is that few of the agencies encourage a more participatory style of operation, the majority operating out of a "social services" mentality which emphasizes the passivity and dependence of older adults. What is required from providers is a more inclusive mode of operation which values the contribution of this subpopulation and which develops programs cooperatively to heighten relevance.

An outstanding model of nonformal education controlled by older adults is embodied in the U3A movement. Not only is the pedagogy developed by older adults but the administration and networking are also carefully managed by them too. But even this exemplary agency has its problems, the chief of which is its failure to attract people outside of the white middle-class majority.

CHAPTER 7

Learning for Older Adults in Social Institutions

As stressed in previous chapters, learning can occur in a variety of contexts and in a variety of modes — as an individual (both self-directed and formally structured), in a group, in organizations, in communities, in social institutions (Smith et al., 1990). In this chapter, attention is focussed upon social institutions in which older adults spend much of their lives and upon emergent learning. The term *institution* is used here in its sociological sense to include private and public systems in which people conduct their lives. More particularly, Blackledge and Hunt (1985, pp.64–65) refer to social institutions as "problem-solving mechanisms" which perform certain crucial "functions" for society. In this case, we are examining institutions which enable older adults to be contributing members of society and the ways in which learning intersects with this socializing function of the institution.

As part of the framework for understanding how older adults might engage in learning through selected social institutions — the family, the church, the media, the workplace and the community — the concept of structural lag, discussed in chapter 4, is pertinent because it illustrates how the convergence or divergence of pathways of education, work and leisure may relate to a person's lifecourse. In this instance, for the older adult, a stereotype is often projected that paid work should play a less prominent role, that education be a social nicety and that leisure be freely indulged in. Unfortunately, choices are more limited than this scenario suggests, especially for those part of an "underclass" in the political economy (Phillipson, 1998). Older adults form a significant portion of an underclass related to poverty and consequent fewer options for living.

Social institutions provide people with opportunities to engage in social behaviors in each of the realms of education, work and leisure. They are sites of learning from daily life in which informal learning is ascendant and formal and nonformal learning is less visible. In each case, older adults have differential opportunities and constraints associated with their relative status and access to power (Biggs, 1993).

LEARNING WITHIN THE FAMILY

The family traditionally has been the fundamental unit of socialization in all societies but it is not commonly analyzed in terms of its learning capacity for older adults. It has a crucial role in social reproduction where the transmission of values and social norms are passed from generation to generation. The interdependence of most individuals in functional families suggests an active interplay between adults and adults, and adults and children across generations. Quite obviously, the experiential mode of learning prevails (Boud & Miller, 1996; Kolb, 1984) but a fuller range of learning approaches would also be evident.

The location of older adults as seniors (sometimes patriarchs and matriarchs) in the family structure provides them with expected educative roles as disseminators of family and cultural histories, role models (guides) and mentors. But as Riley and Riley (1994, p.31) point out, these expectations either can be made void or further enhanced by the existence of reconstituted families where relationships and roles are more indeterminate. So, the best we can say is that in many instances these educative roles exist but are not assumed.

Jerrome (1998) comments that to understand relationships in the later-life family (i.e. those families who are beyond the childbearing years and have sent their children into the world), we need to acknowledge huge changes which have affected the family in the last 100 years. These changes can be grouped as demographic, technological, legal, ideological and economic. Here are a couple of examples to consider. Demographically, the rates of mortality have fallen, family size has shrunk, age at marriage and the number of children born to each family varies. These factors alter the age distribution within families and the consequent roles of older people in a more complex array of relationships. From an economic viewpoint, rising affluence and the existence of welfare in some nations allows for more choice in family relationships. As a consequence, relationships between elderly parents and their adult children are more governed by sentiment than obligation (Jerrome, 1998).

The ability of older adults, usually as grandparents, to play the role of transmitter of local and social knowledge (Kolb, 1984) is obviously affected by particular family configurations and the degree of communication between family members. The prospect of older people having more discretionary time to spend with their children and children's children is tempered by the availability of the younger members to engage in face-to-face dialogue. Sometimes, when face-to-face contact is not possible, then advanced technologies such as e-mail enable this communication to occur.

There is little doubt that mentoring by older adults of younger persons is widespread though more commonly associated with work than family. Mentoring comes in many guises— guide, friend, counselor—and is defined by Carmin (1988) as:

> a complex, interactive process occurring between individuals of differing levels of experience and expertise which incorporates interpersonal or psychological development, career and/or educational development and socialization functions into the relationship (cited in Jarvis, 2001, p.86)

Mentoring is generally considered to entail a formalized scheme though this need not necessarily be the case. In the Maori context in New Zealand, on the *marae* (meeting house and surrounds), it is common for a *kaumatua* (older man) to sit with his *mokopuna* (grandchildren) and speak of tribal customs and practices. Inside the meeting house itself, young children watch senior members of the tribe recite *whakapapa* (genealogy)

religious time and the habits of a lifetime have persisted. Another plausible reason is the proximity of death to third agers and the more intense interest in the meaning of life which is purported to occur at this stage of living (Fisher, 1993; Jarvis, 2001).

Aside from religious knowledge and spiritual reinforcement which occurs in a church setting, older adults also establish networks of people to whom they can relate on a systematic basis to achieve social goals. Quite often, the formal service on a Sunday is the tip of the iceberg of opportunities for members of a congregation to learn about themselves and their relationship to the universe. Less formal and more social occasions quite often accrue for learning in a church environment. While the formal service is traditionally modeled on the lecture format of "expert-novice", in modern churches the relationship is increasingly "teacher-participant" as services become more collaborative and interactive.

The church is undoubtedly a very important social institution for many older adults in an increasingly secular world. It not only can meet spiritual needs but it also can be a locale of social networks and learning. Churches are underrated places for adult learning to occur. On the one hand, a sensitive spiritual leader/teacher can help older adults to retain knowledge of a religious kind, challenge people's beliefs about life, and provide encouragement to engage in social action to improve the world. On the other, effective leaders can also foster a learning community, be a facilitator (Rogers, 1983) to spearhead collaborative learning.

The potential of churches to become more effective institutions of learning for all generations is also understated. They can be sites of intergenerational conflict in terms of the mode of teaching (young people quite often want to engage in more interactive experiential learning) but have great potential for interaction across generations. If hierarchically structured services (including sermons) were opened for more input from the congregation and connected more closely with real life, then numbers in church attendance might again climb. In practice, educators need to take into account the potentially strong influence of spirituality and the church and work alongside older adults in adopting practices which support their personal and social development.

THE MEDIA AS A SOCIAL INSTITUTION

The phrase "the media" refers to a range of public communicators of information to a citizenry including newspapers, magazines, television, the cinema and the internet. Aside from allowing for direct contact of people with older adults, the media provide societies with the language and conceptions about aging and "old people". In labeling theory, the media bestow images and myths of what it means to be an elder in society (Blaikie, 1999). They have the power to define the range of acceptable behavior and to control what the populace sees as normative and deviant for older adults. As an instrument of the state, the media can disseminate "official" views of older adult issues and recommend to people what they should think (Gramsci, 1971).

The media have the potential to domesticate (Freire, 1984) or to challenge orthodoxy, to help develop critical thinkers (Brookfield, 1987). Unfortunately, the "official" history of old age is very much a history of decrepitude, passivity, dependence and enfeeblement (Blaikie, 1999). Media have helped create this set of myths. As a case in point, small-screen portrayals have not tended to project a positive image of older adults; older people are less visible on screen than their proportions of the population, despite the fact they make a sizeable and loyal viewing public.

Blaikie argues that with the advent of consumer culture, business has woken up to the commercial potential of the mature market. But there is also the emergence of the third age of personal fulfillment. The two trends combine to create an aging population that focuses on leisure and lifestyle. Popular photo magazines such as *the American People Weekly* are replete with glamorous shots of older people who have altered their bodies with plastic surgery, facelifts, liposuction etc. Joan Collins at 70 is a delectable sight and Cliff Richard in his mid-60s is fitness personified. Blaikie comments: "A positive imagery is winning the day, one that emphasizes the maintenance of youth, fitness, and discernment through leisure until well past the point of retirement" (1999, p.108). He is left to ask whether this positive portrayal has gone too far. With respect to Laslett's third and fourth ages, Young and Schuller (cited in Blaikie, 1999, p.110) observe:

> Elevating the third age—is only done by treading down the fourth. The labeling problem is wished on to even older and more defenceless people.

Clearly the media have an ethical responsibility to project realistic images of what it means to be an older adult. They should include both the optimistic and pessimistic views of human achievement and behavior; they should portray the possibilities of older age as well as its limitations.

In chapter 10 of *Learning to Grow Older and Bolder* (1999), Carlton and Soulsby explain how in the UK information technology and broadcast media have provided adults generally, and older adults especially, with the flexibility of time and space to pursue further learning. Such media for distance learning blurs the line between informal learning for its own sake and more instrumental learning with qualifications attached. The new technologies of information and technology deliver the following prospects for older adults:

- Aids in the home, such as automatic control and security systems
- Information, advice and guidance, including health, civic and public affairs
- Communications with family, friends and agencies at a distance
- Entertainment and creative interests
- Learning programmes, whether vocational, qualification bearing or informal (p.59).

These authors point out that "technology contributes to maintaining their quality of life and independent living, especially for those who are isolated socially or geographically, or are frail or disabled" (1999, p.59).

With respect to broadcasting, radio and television play a key role in the lives of older adults. The British Audience Research Bureau statistics (cited in Carlton & Soulsby, 1999, p.60) indicate that for people over 65 the average time spent watching television is 36 hours a week, significantly more than for younger generations. In both radio and television more attention has been paid to issues affecting older adults and some more rebellious characters have been portrayed in programs such as *One Foot in the Grave* and *Waiting for God*. Hence, the media can themselves reflect the contradictions of aging—continuing with deficit stereotypes of aging on the one hand; demonstrating proactive and deviant characters on the other.

In the American environment, Timmermann (1998) further discusses the role of information technology in older adult learning. Although around 30% of older adults between 55 and 74 own a computer, 14% of Internet users are over the age of 50. Not surprisingly, she reports that older people who participate in on-line adult education programs rise significantly with the level of formal education and socioeconomic status. The barriers to participation, discussed in chapter 5, also apply in this context to older adults. In particular, access to computers, sympathetic instruction on their use in a noncompetitive situation, and attention to affective factors are all positive ways of overcoming misperceptions and reluctance to engage in e-learning.

The SeniorNet movement, strong in the USA and other Western countries, is an international nonprofit organization. It leads older adults in learning how to effectively use computers and on-line facilities. SeniorNet Learning Centers constitute an excellent case of a successful peer-taught instructional program for older adults. Timmermann (1998, p.65) identifies three factors as salient in this success story:

- Small classes with a dedicated space and time for instruction;
- One-to-one tutoring with computer coaches using a clear curriculum allowing for self-pacing;

- Using peer instructors who are volunteers and who themselves have completed train-the-trainers programs.

Finally, she ruminates on the relative lack of success of distance learning which demands a certain level of self-directed learner with access to suitable facilities. Just as any adults vary in their preferences for instruction or self-study, older adults, dependent on their material circumstances, will have differential access to computer facilities and capability to use them effectively.

Practitioners should be conscious of the ways in which various media help shape the contours of older adults' lives. A passive acceptance of the hegemonic influence of media by professionals working with older people is unlikely to change lives for the better. It is incumbent on educators and carers in communities to question the influence of media on older adults' lives and work towards developing a more critical stance where the older people themselves make more active decisions on the use of media.

COMMUNITY-BASED INITIATIVES

The wider field of adult and community education has many tales of how community collaboration and resolve have overcome social problems in diverse locations. In some instances, the community has been marginalized and subjected to oppression resultant from the forces of the political economy. These kinds of community-based initiatives have developed from a more radical pedagogy (Freire, 1984).

Success stories have been documented in such varying locations as an inner city suburb in Edinburgh (Kirkwood & Kirkwood, 1989), popular education in Canada (Gatt-Fly, 1996) and experimental education at Staten Island Community College, New York (Shor, 1980). Added to this list would be the emancipatory work of the Highlander Research and Education Center in Tennessee which has supported the rights of oppressed peoples in the American South to a decent way of life (Gaventa,

1980; Horton). Yet, curiously, in my search for a comparable older adults' movement, the cupboard is nearly bare. In the last-mentioned case of Highlander, many older adults were involved in literacy work with black Americans to encourage them to read and write, especially for voter registration. But aside from sporadic episodes of occasional activism by older adults, the radical pedagogical context remains new territory to be explored.

From a liberal perspective, older adults have been involved in community education provision. In Auckland, for example, the English for Speakers of Other Languages (ESOL) Home Tutors Scheme uses many older adults to work alongside new immigrants as the latter try to learn a new language and acculturate to a new way of life. In some instances, older adults (as volunteers) are mentoring older adults (as new immigrant learners). At the local Takapuna Citizens' Advice Bureau (CAB) on the North Shore of Auckland the director is a woman in her mid 80s and her supporters are older adults from their late 50s onwards. These examples illustrate that many socially oriented (not for profit) agencies are propped up by the efforts of older volunteers (Caro & Bass, 1995).

The British government has been trying to encourage greater collaboration between different levels of government, including the very localized. In 1998 the *Better Government for Older People* (BGOP) Programme was started with the support of the Local Authorities Research Consortium. The University of Warwick, together with Help the Aged, Age Concern England, Anchor Trust and the Carnegie Third Age Programme, sought greater coordination at both national and local levels. The principal agenda has been to improve the quality of life for older people, using a lifelong learning needs approach. One instance has been the Wolverhampton Metropolitan Borough Council's objectives stated as:

- Increasing the influence of older people in service planning
- Improving the physical environment
- Increasing opportunities for participation in social, educational and community activities

- Improving employment opportunities for old people
- Supporting older people as volunteers and in intergenerational work
- Improving information and choice
- Promoting positive attitudes to old age
  (Carlton & Soulsby, 1999, pp.64–65).

Quite clearly, the potential for older adults to participate in community-based initiatives is virtually unlimited. In these instances, the nonformal and informal learning patterns of seniors come to the fore. Practitioners are well advised to bring such opportunities to the attention of older people so that they benefit as individuals and the local community also prospers as a result.

THE WORKPLACE AS
A SOCIAL INSTITUTION

In Riley and Riley's conception of the lifecourse (1994), work is forever present in our lives. While Laslett's second age has traditionally been the main platform for paid work (though for some, a lifetime of unemployment persists), the third age stereotypically has been characterized by increasing leisure and reduced or no paid work. This situation presupposes an individual's ability to be economically self-sufficient and/or be a recipient of a government or private-funded pension. While this may be the case for people in lifetime stable careers, in the (post)modern world there is considerably more uncertainty for guaranteed work or work at a sustainable level.

For older adults, the reconfiguration of work has had dire consequences for those at the margins of the workforce who enter later life with few financial resources and little capacity to undertake meaningful part-time work (Thomson, 1999). On the other hand, those older adults who have benefited from secure employment and generous superannuation schemes, the future is much brighter, coupled with the more assured financial base and the capability to work further, if necessary. In short, there are differential work and income opportunities available to different categories of older adults, dependent on such variables as social class, gender, race/ethnicity and geographical location. The terrain of work is uneven, rugged and volatile. Those adults with more extensive educational backgrounds are much more likely to sustain themselves when economic times get tough.

The structure of the labor force is changing, aligned to governments' desires to have an "up-skilled" workforce capable of competing internationally in the global marketplace. As explained in chapter 4, prevalent patterns of full-time paid work are not equally distributed throughout society. Some subgroups suffer from meagre access to sustained employment. Quite typically, marginalized groups, including significant proportions of older workers, are disenfranchised from a secure career path, thus jeopardizing their continuing financial security. They are especially vulnerable in national economies where alternative cheap labor is readily available and where public policy encourages privatization rather than governmental provision of assured work or pensions in retirement. Hence, the fruits of "retirement" are dispersed unevenly and this fragmentation of economic resources can have dire consequences for an older adult underclass in society (Phillipson, 1998).

Given the above scenario, what are the implications for older adults? First, the traditional approach to "retirement" needs an overhaul as do the educational programs geared towards its successful attainment. Not everyone gets to retire; not everyone wants to! Some may opt for a combination of part-time paid work; some voluntary work; some planned leisure. The move from "worker" to "nonworker" is no longer clearcut. Certainly, for women, the pattern of employment is usually different from the linear path of men. As identified by Lamdin and Fugate (1997, p.148):

> Some can't retire because their unpaid work never ends. These people are mostly women whose work has been in the home and

the community, neither of which gives them a pension or the option of formally calling it quits.

So, preretirement education will need to be more individually based as the pattern of retirement has become less regular. The exception to this scenario would be those groups of older people who come from collectivist cultures where cooperation rather than competition is the underlying predominant modality of activity. Here, a more empathetic inductive approach, based on a collaborative investigation of retirement themes, would better serve the practitioner and target group (Freire, 1984).

Learning during retirement or the later years of work will relate to the pattern of work and leisure that a person can fashion, related to social and material conditions. White middle-class adults may find organizations such as U3A useful in meeting learning needs; others will need to look at other groups or clubs to match their pocketbooks and interests. In the arena of volunteering, many older adults find fulfillment in meaningful work and social relationships and the potential for further learning is significant (Swindell, 1997) as discussed in the next section.

VOLUNTEERING AS
A SOCIAL CONSTRUCTION

Lamdin and Fugate (1997) in the American context discuss the importance of volunteering to individuals and to society. Older adults throughout the USA are being trained as aides in classrooms, docents in museums and galleries, volunteers in medicine and as paraprofessionals in social agencies. Importantly, much of this volunteering enables the older adult to use previously acquired knowledge and skills in a contributive way for their own and the community's benefit, as in the examples in SeniorNet and U3A movements. Whereas previously women in their middle years were the backbone of the volunteering stock, their need to enter the workforce has made them less available and older adults have tended to step into this task

(Caro & Bass, 1995). These authors found that the groups of people beyond 55 who were most likely to volunteer to be:

- Women
- Those with education beyond high school
- Those with professional or technical skills
- Those in good health, and
- Those active in religion
    (1995, p.77).

The economic and political context of volunteering should not be under-estimated. While on the one hand, volunteering can provide much needed value to both the giver and the receiver, it does, on the other, have the potential to displace paid workers from the workforce. When governments, as in the case of New Zealand, see many voluntary, nongovernmental and welfare organizations sustained by competent volunteers, what incentive is there to provide decent funding to replace this work? In the health sector, in particular, voluntary labor has often been used when many would argue for sufficient funding from the state. Hence, the socioeconomic context of older adult volunteering is never neutral—voluntary organizations, volunteers and practitioners should be aware of the larger social context in which their activity resides.

The arena of older adult volunteering in community services, including institutional and community care, is especially poignant. The area of "community care" is contentious in that it is sometimes portrayed as the opposite of "institutional care" (which may have connotations of containment and social control of older adults). Community care is often a pseudonym for family care where once again women's work and potential exploitation is to the fore (Biggs, 1993, p.124). In the case of institutional care, older adults are the recipients, the cared for; in community services, older adults are more often the givers, the carers. The line between "carer" and "cared for" is not strongly demarcated. The line between autonomy and dependency is equally thin. This is the same line between Laslett's (1989) third and fourth age learners.

At a political level, volunteerism can have a significant

impact on society as public figures like Barry Goldwater and Jimmy Carter demonstrate. Third-agers can be a very persuasive force in politics in issues such as affirmative action, environmental issues, gay rights and educational reform, though seldom in unison. Older citizens often value the opportunity to advocate for a cause which will make for a better world for their (grand)children to inherit. Finally, Lamdin and Fugate point out that much volunteering is nonorganized where "invisible" people make important contributions to society without seeking recognition or reward.

CONCLUSION

This chapter has explored some of the ways in which older adults as learners engage with social institutions, both private and public. A central message is that in the daily lives of older adults they get involved with many different social institutions and networks which have an impact on their potential to learn. Learning in these institutions is a crucial factor in their finding meaning in their lives as they move from the second age (usually focussing on work and family responsibilities) into the third age (purportedly marked by autonomy and creativity), into the fourth (characterized by decline and decrepitude).

In the domains of family, church, community, the media, the workplace and volunteering, there is considerable learning that occurs, usually though not exclusively, in the informal learning mode. The social institutions with which many older adults engage are undervalued as sources of learning, both expressive and instrumental. In volunteering, particularly, older adults find a way of contributing to society, sustaining their own well-being and simultaneously injecting a huge labor force into social welfare and community services.

CHAPTER 8

Contemporary Issues for Older Adults' Learning

The overall direction of this book has been that of analyzing the convergence of learning in older adulthood with the complex realities of elders' lives. Learning does not exist free of contextual factors, free of the complexities of people's existence. On the contrary, it springs out of the issues and concerns which confront older adults wherever they may work, learn and re-create. While the potential issues which face specific groups of older adults are limitless, I have selected some major issues which have a definite impact on the scope of learning in later life. These issues may not be exclusive to older adults but are more commonly experienced by them, thus demanding some kind of response from themselves and practitioners.

STRUCTURAL LAG AND OLDER ADULTS' RESPONSES

In chapter 4, I employed Riley and Riley's (1994) framework of an age-integrated depiction of social structures to argue for a new way of encapsulating the normative lifecourse of individuals in Western societies. Instead of the traditional sequential stages of education, work and leisure, the model presented by the Rileys is much more complex, exciting and challenging, especially for adults in the third age.

No previous cohort of older adults has benefited from advanced technologies of communication and of health care to the extent of the baby-boomers now experiencing or entering this stage of life. Greater numbers of older adults will soon pervade societal structures with heightened expectations of participation in most realms of social life. Nor has educational opportunity been as readily available to this emerging group who, in general terms, have higher standards of education and living than prior generations. However, this generalization needs to be tempered by differential opportunity for specific groups, particularly those with few financial resources.

The concept of structural lag is based on the assumption that social structures lag behind people's lived experiences. As a case for discussion, I use the world of work. Under an age-integrated model, sustained meaningful work could be better afforded to greater proportions of older adults. Spreading work across all ages, as the model suggests, would enable more elders to undertake part-time jobs until later in the lifecourse and provide industries with a chance to employ more seniors as mentors for less experienced workers. On-the-job education could be used more extensively. The concurrent issue of a realistic wage for older workers would need to be negotiated as part of an overall package to retain their expertise. The impact on the individual older person of a planned reduction in work hours (as opposed to a sudden stoppage) would be ego-enhancing and the other areas of life for that person (leisure, family commitments, club membership, continuing education) could occupy better balance. At a national level, the flow-on effects in the economy should be positively felt, as a more motivated workforce tends to improve productivity. In social and cultural spheres, the benefits should also be manifested in keener social engagement and greater participation in learning activities across all ages (Riley & Riley, 1994).

This new social structure is unlikely to emerge in a systematic way unless embraced by governments and linked to social policy and a learning society. It is more likely to emerge in more economically advanced societies as a result of pressure-group action on specific cultural fronts. Education has a role to raise the awareness of *all* society to changing norms and expectations as social structures (sometimes reluctantly) change. There is the potential through education to help mobilize older citizens to advocate for changes (such as having more relevant and convenient educational programs) in organizations, in local and central governments.

Arguably, older adults currently have a golden opportunity to effect real change if they work collectively toward social action to improve their own well-being and those of future generations. Rather than accepting the epithet of the "frail" and "inconsequential", senior citizens can assume more active roles to target change from a liberatory framework (Alinsky, 1971; Shor, 1980; Mayo, 1997). Evolutionary or slow change supports structural lag; revolutionary or radical change supports structural change.

Practitioners could undertake more active strategies to support older adults in initiating social change in addition to adjusting to it. Advocates are needed for changing social structures and processes which disadvantage older people so that structural lag does not spoil their life chances.

INDEPENDENCE OR INTERDEPENDENCE?

The adult learning literature is heavily weighted towards concepts which advocate for continuing independence throughout life. For example, the notion of self-directed learning is based on the assumption that the epitome of adult learning involves self-reliant individualists who can plan, implement and evaluate their own learning (Mezirow, 1981, 1984; Knowles, 1984; Brookfield, 1986; Caffarella, 2001). In the adult development area, most (male) conceptions of the successful adjuster to life's vicissitudes are those who demonstrate a mature, self-mastery of life's tasks (Havighurst, 1972; Fisher, 1993) in a largely independent mode.

On the other hand, many of the earlier notions of autonomy and self-responsibility advocated through humanists, including those writing from a developmental perspective, have been forthrightly challenged by feminist theorists who argue the gender (and sometimes class) bias of such viewpoints. Instead, they promote the view that in much of life it is interdependence which is the hallmark of human coexistence (Belenky et al., 1986; Drewery, 1991; Thompson; 1983; Sheared & Sissel, 2001; Ryan, 2001). For instance, Drewery argues, in terms of developmental patterns, that women very typically seek interdependence in their lives rather than independence. She argues we should stop seeing independence as the norm or pinnacle of human relationships and look for ways in which people cooperate and help one another achieve goals.

A balanced view of human development would incorporate elements of both traditions. For older adults reflecting on their lives, men would probably observe that in their younger years they were more likely to have assumed roles which emphasized independence (e.g. breadwinner for the family) and women would note interdependence as more characteristic of their behavior (e.g. mother as carer in the home). Men more often appear in instrumental roles; women in expressive ones. As age increases, the chance for both genders to diversify their gender-based roles also increases. Men can assume more expressive occupations, largely freed from responsibility as a primary provider (though this situation of sole provider is now much less common than previously); women can "hand over" more household chores and perhaps veer away from domesticity (Gerson, 1985).

Given the enormous range of lifestyles available in contemporary life, few patterns of life (or developmental tasks) can any longer be assumed based on gender and age. Arber and Ginn's (1995) anthology, *Connecting Gender and Ageing*, points to the complexities of changing roles in later life, related to gender. In short, the "old rules" no longer apply; the Western world is re-creating the possibilities of what it means to "grow old". We can be both independent and interdependent in our lives related to the diverse roles we play and the multiple subjectivities triggered by them (Ryan, 2001).

The role of practitioners is to be open to new pathways of combinations of independence and interdependence. It is understandable that educators assume gender-specific behaviors for older men and women respectively but we should realize that to do so reinforces the status quo (which heavily disadvantages women) and provides little opportunity for either sex to diversify life roles.

DEMANDS OF
TECHNOLOGICAL INNOVATION

How many older adults do you see using mobile phones in public places? How many senior citizens have not used a computer before? How many grandparents get their grandkids to set up or adjust their new appliances in the home? The answers to these questions will vary but the likelihood is that there are large numbers proportionately of older adults who need "mentoring" by younger people in embracing new technologies.

There is a prevalent image of older adults being set in their ways to the extent that they avoid engaging with new technological demands (Timmermann, 1998). There is undoubtedly some truth in this observation. My son is much more keen and adept at installing the new video machine than I am. It is the *attitude* rather than the lack of skills which is more at the heart of the matter. The attitude, in turn, has been induced, in part at least, by increasing caution and rigidity of seniors (Glass, 1996) and the fear of "not keeping up" but also by societal expectation of disengagement and elders' belief in this myth.

The stereotype of older adult disengagement from new technology is exposed as simplistic in such innovations as Seniornet, as discussed in chapter 7. In effect, a "community of learners" is established without the necessity of participants actually physically meeting one another but being able to communicate over common interests. The challenge is succinctly expressed by Timmermann (1998, p.62), in summarizing the characteristics of on-line users:

> Paralleling the statistics of the characteristics of older people who participate in adult education programs, computer ownership and online participation rise significantly with the level of formal education and socio-economic status.

While the "good news" is that the number of male online participants is more than the average for adult education participation, the "bad news" is that social class, and probably ethnicity, play a part in determining who has access to this technology for learning. The word "probably" is inserted here because through my contacts in Auckland city, I know that there is considerable overlap in membership between U3A and Seniornet. U3A is almost exclusively a white middle-class phenomenon in New Zealand (Swindell, 1999). Seniornet is highly likely to share the same characteristics of membership.

One way forward in promoting the availability and utility of computers is via pubic-private partnerships as described by Timmermann (1998). Given that computer companies can see older adults as a new market to be expanded (through older citizen's supposed increased leisure time and discretionary funds), they can forge links with salient organizations with whom older adults associate. For example, the Community Technology Seminars organized by Microsoft and the American Association of Retired Persons (AARP) provide opportunities for seniors to learn about computers in a relatively nonthreatening environment.

Many interesting studies have been conducted to investigate older adults familiarity with and use of computers. Studies looking into older people's reactions to computer usage have included a focus on the behavior of different cohorts of older adults (Morrell, Mayhorn and Bennett, 2000), computer use among elderly persons in long-term care facilities (Namazi and McClintic, 2003), relationships with psychological well-being (Chen and Persson, 2002) and the extent of Internet use among older adult learners (Cody, Dunn, Hoppin and Wendt, 1999).

In an article which presents some baseline data on who are Internet users in the USA, Fox et al. (2001) point out that while senior citizens comprise 13% of the US population, they constitute only 4% of the US Internet population. Those who do engage in regular Internet use do so primarily for communicating with family, researching health information and to track financial investments. However, these authors refer to "a wide gray gap" (p.2) because while 56% of all Americans go online, only

15% over the age of 65 have access to the Internet. There appears to be a "senior elite" who are enthusiastic surfers, often coaxed by children and grandchildren to go online. Such "wired seniors" are characterized, in comparison with offline peers, to be married, highly educated, and enjoying relatively high retirement incomes. More senior men than senior women use the Internet (Fox et al., 2001, p.2). This portrayal of participants mirrors trends in adult education participation more generally i.e. those who already have, get more.

A study of "silver surfers" was conducted by Cody, Dunn, Hoppin and Wendt (1999) in which 292 older adult learners (averaging 80 years of age) were recruited to learn about computer technologies, including surfing the Internet. The investigators were particularly concerned with training issues of older adults in Internet use in this four-month program. The majority of the sample had hardly any experience with computers (57%); 87% had had no experience with the Internet. Prior research had identified several variables as significant in relation to the training of older adults: computer anxiety, computer efficacy (the belief in one's capability to effectively use a computer), attitude toward aging and social support (Cody et al., 1999, p.271). These researchers ascertained that those who learned to surf the Internet had more positive attitudes to aging, higher levels of perceived social support and higher levels of connectivity. In their reflections on the project the researchers observe that "to be successful—programs should focus on reducing anxiety and building efficacy (and do so early) and feature lessons phrased optimistically and in encouraging formats" (p.281).

In a comparative study between young and older adults' use of the Internet, Chen and Persson (2002) investigated the link between Internet use and psychological well-being. They observed in their sample of 396 that in comparison with older nonusers, the older Internet users tended to be healthier, better educated and had more financial resources and they reported greater levels of psychological well-being. In comparison with younger Internet users their psychological well-being was also more highly rated. Again, these findings confirm the trend that older adults who engage in fruitful activity tend to benefit significantly in their personal lives.

In a study which focussed on World Wide Web use in 550 middle-aged (40–59), young-old (60–74) and old-old (75–92) adults in Michigan, Morell, Mayhorn and Bennett (2000, p.175) ascertained the following results:

(a) there are distinct age and demographic differences in individuals who use the Web;

(b) middle-aged and older Web users are similar in their use patterns;

(c) the two primary predictors for not using the Web are lack of access to a computer and lack of knowledge about the Web;

(d) old-old adults have the least interest in using the Web compared with middle-aged and young-old adults;

(e) the primary content areas in learning how to use the Web are learning how to use electronic mail and accessing health information and information about traveling for pleasure.

None of these findings is really surprising but they do confirm that the older one is, the less likely it is that there will be familiarity with computers and their benefits.

Namazi and McClintic (2003) looked into 24 elderly persons residing in long-term care facilities and tracked through their participation patterns in a computer-class designed specifically to teach them to become independent in operating a computer. After 15 months, only five persisted in their use of computers. The researchers analyzed categories of obstacles that may have led to discontinuation as follows:

• Physical and cognitive (e.g. memory limitations)
• Personal (e.g. optimistic and pessimistic orientations)
• Hardware/software and other technological factors (e.g. computers not designed for use by frail persons)
• Organizational (e.g. inadequate numbers of computers)
• Physical environmental (e.g. lack of privacy or personal space)

The authors conclude that the elderly persons enjoyed the computer activities and the inherent challenges but that more attention in future would need to be paid to logistical factors.

The responses of older adults to new technologies is obviously varied. Early adopters tend to be those with a solid educational base, better economic resources and a more opportunistic attitude (See Everett Rogers, 1983, for an elaborated explanation on the diffusion of innovation and the characteristics of early adopters). It is too simplistic to argue that most older adults resist new technologies—much more evidence is needed around the circumstances of choice and the material conditions in which older adults live. This point is echoed in Carlton and Soulby's (1999) analysis of potential Information Technology users among older citizens in the UK.

Although the majority of older adults struggle to get to grips with new technologies, it is seldom related to learning capacity. Many of the reasons discussed in chapter 5 for older adults not participating in educational programs are also true for reluctance to engage with innovation. Practitioners can assist older adults to remove barriers to this kind of learning and be stronger supporters of training and development for older adults in the technological domain.

CULTURAL VARIATION IN RESPONSES TO AGING

When on a visit to Malaysia in the late 1990s I was astounded to learn that a colleague with whom I was sharing a car was about to retire at the tender age of 55. He looked much too young and vibrant to give up paid work! The Malaysian Government requires that public servants "retire" at this age, presumably to allow for younger workers to enter the public service. The reality for the individual was not traumatic—retire from public service on the Friday; start in private practice on the Monday in a similar role. What this vignette alerted me to was the difference in the national outlooks and policies of our two respective countries. In New Zealand compulsory retirement was being abandoned; in the more "managed economy" of Malaysia, the state needed to intervene to try to ensure a greater distribution of paid work across ages.

In the above example, the concept of *culture* has been equated with national interests, though this is only one possible interpretation of what "cultural" might mean. In that same country, no doubt indigenous Malays, Chinese and Indian ethnic groups would understand the world differently though each group would probably revere elderly people more so than in the West. But as Blaikie (1999) has explained, it is too easy to argue that modernization has caused a diminution in the role and status of elderly in Western countries—"the roles and statuses of older people in the family, employment, and civil society more generally have always been multifaceted" (1999, p.55).

If we interpret "cultural" to be "ethnic" differences in responses to aging, then these are undoubtedly significant. As an illustration, in the New Zealand scene with which I am most familiar, the worldviews of Pakeha and Maori are very different on many measures. The individualistic stance of most Europeans to any social issue contrasts with the collective, cooperative stance of most Maori. The case of aging is no exception. In a forthright article, Maaka (1993) analyzes some of the salient differences. His observations include this generalization:

> One of the more obvious differences between Pakeha and Maori aged . . . is that instead of slipping into quiet retirement many kaumatua become super-active and are busier than they have ever been in their whole lives (p.223).

Kaumatua is a generic term for older adults in traditional settings. While Maaka assumes the disengagement of most Pakeha, possibly an erroneous belief, the main point of his remark is to stress that in the Maori world, older adults tend to grow in stature as a result of aging. He links this to their enhanced responsibilities associated with leadership expectations. Older Maori are presumed to have considerable life experience which needs to be shared with the entire extended family. As Maaka (1993, p.222) explains:

> No self-respecting Maori organization can operate effectively without its *tuaraa* (backbone) — its supporting kaumatua or group of kaumatua.

In effect, the roles of elderly Maori expand in range and importance so that their expertise can be shared with the collective.

In comparison, Pakeha society historically has tended to constrain rather than expand the duties of older adults (though, arguably, this trend is changing). Certainly, care for frail European elderly is more often arranged through a health provider than through family members (Green, 1993). Few Maori elders end up in rest homes because care of kaumatua would be seen as a direct family responsibility. Perhaps the only valid generalizations for Pakeha are that inherited models of relating to older adults were transplanted from the UK and elsewhere in Europe to New Zealand and some of these persist; that there is little recognition at a public level given to older people for what they do.

Undoubtedly, cultural differences between and within societies account for many different patterns of how older adults themselves behave and how people at large respond to them. One way practitioners can deal with this situation is to relate to others who have experienced such cultures first hand and to read critically about norms of particular ethnic groups. Plenty of professional seminars on cultural dynamics are available through public continuing education programs as well as through more formal, academic study. In short, practitioners need to adopt an active attitude to finding out more of cultural practices as well as reflecting on their own behaviors with older adults in varying cultural contexts.

DEALING WITH DEATH AND DYING

In Laslett's (1989) fourth age of decrepitude, people are terminally ill and preparing for death. It is at this stage that hopefully Erikson's (1950) integrity is to the fore rather than despair. Certainly, it is a time when individuals reflect on their lives (assuming still alert mental faculties) and how they have contributed to self, family and society. The importance of reminiscence in reconstructing positive self-images prior to death should not be underestimated, as others such as Merriam (1985) and Jarvis (2001) have remarked. It allows individuals the opportunity to see their lives as worthwhile and contributing positively to others.

The processes of grief, loss, and dying have been well documented elsewhere (e.g. Kubler-Ross, 1970). Historically and culturally, the process of dying and death has been treated in many different ways. In a lifelong learning society, there are still educative tasks to be completed in relation to death and dying. For the dying individual, wise counsel from carers and spiritual leaders can help a person find peace. For the carers, there is ongoing need to keep a broader perspective on life while channeling most effort into caring strategies. Education to help carers to develop better relationships with family members and skills in caring can be learned in clinical settings or in hospices. In the realm of early childhood education, the claim is made that teaching and caring go hand in hand (May, 1990)—the same appears to be true at the other end of life.

The service and associated events connected to death can be a major learning experience in themselves. This is certainly the situation in the Maori context where a *tangihanga* (extended funeral service and rituals) provides the opportunity for people in a public forum to express their sentiments for the deceased and renew their relationships with the living surrounding the loved one. The entire event constitutes a public recognition of the importance of that family member to the wider tribe, a meeting point for different groups known to the deceased, a spiritual linking of life with death as well as a celebration among the living for the individual as part of community. The tangihanga is a fully experiential event which readily fits with the learning cycle promoted by learning theorists (Kolb, 1984).

Outside the Maori context, from my own experiencing of funerals in different cultural settings, there now appears to be a greater concentration on the value of life and celebrating a person's life rather than on the grief and anguish associated with death. The broader range of funeral services also allows for more individuality to be expressed, including the incorporation of humor, alongside seriousness. Learning occurs in the cognitive and affective domains wherein we reconstruct our earlier experiences of relating to dying people and anticipate experiences around the death of others (Dewey, 1938).

As practitioners, we can become more knowledgeable about the dying process in addition to thoughtfully reflecting on our own responses to losing a loved one. Again, opportunities abound for learning more about our own grieving and loss, about learning how to care for others facing imminent death, and for learning how to better care for carers.

SOCIAL POLICY CHALLENGES
FOR NATION-STATES

The issue of social policy development and implementation in relation to older adults is important to all sectors of society, least of all for the reason that sooner or later the vast majority of people will enter the third age. It is naive to look at policies affecting only older adults because humans are interconnected across generations. Yet on the other hand, not to concentrate on senior citizens will lead to inevitable dilution of purpose. Hence, there is always a dilemma of focus in assessing social policy on older adults in any context.

I would like to suggest that in examining the topic of learning in later life from a social policy perspective that a framework be used which works from the inside out i.e. we look for direct and immediate policy proclamations and consequences first. Later we study more generic social policy statements (e.g. on housing, women, health, work, and law) for their impact on older people. Further, while a host of organizations can create policy related to older adults (e.g. local councils; social agencies), that initially policies from the state be given preference as an indicator of a nation's commitment to older adults.

The publication *Learning to Grow Older and Bolder* by NIACE in the UK broke new ground as an earnest attempt to map the policy issues surrounding older people in that nation. Its focus was on (social) policy in relation to learning in later life. The content of the policy paper included:

- the fuller context of what learning means to older people;
- some demographic information on the UK scene;
- consideration of participation issues;
- the character of provision for older people through diverse sources such as local authorities, further education, and higher education;
- discussion around other bodies involved in coordinating services for older adults; and
- recommendations for future action.

From my observation, this policy paper treated the entire topic very seriously and in a holistic manner. For the nation of Great Britain, this paper constitutes a major challenge and it is a good start! Other nations are encouraged to follow this exemplar.

While New Zealand always operates on a smaller scale than Britain, it has made attempts in recent government documents to depict the reality of living for older adults (but largely outside the context of lifelong learning). The Government through its ministries has published the following reports since 2001:

- The New Zealand Positive Ageing Strategy 2001 Positive Ageing in New Zealand: Diversity, Participation and Change
- Living Standards of Older New Zealanders: A Summary
- Towards Lifelong Participation and Independence 2002: A Briefing to the Incoming Minister for Senior Citizens
- Health of Older People Strategy 2002

The encouraging aspect of these reports is that fuller attention is being given to the plight of older adults in this society. While no specific document has surfaced regarding learning in

later adulthood in recent years, it is in the hands of adult educators to rectify this situation. They need to argue for policy
formulation to more closely connect the material lives of older
New Zealanders, as indicated with the above reports, to lifelong
learning imperatives.

In addition to government-initiated policy statements, there
are other organizations with explicit roles to play in the lives of
older adults who publish relevant policy. Again, in the New Zealand context, in 2001 Age Concern published a booklet entitled
Ageing is Living: A Guide to Positive Ageing. It includes demographic data, an exploration of myths and realities of aging, key
factors for positive aging, preparing for older age and strategies
for promoting positive aging in the community. At another
level, several city councils (local authorities) have published
policy on older persons. One such example is from Hamilton
City Council (HCC), whose Community Development Department published in 1999, a document called *Older Persons Policy:
Celebrating Life!* The stated purposes of this policy are to:

- Guide HCC actions in addressing the needs of older people in
  Hamilton City
- Provide a framework with which to begin to achieve the vision
  for Hamilton as a city that values people of all ages (p.3).

Hence, we see here a forward-looking local government
prepared to invest in people as well as drains and footpaths.

In essence, what is required is for different sections of communities (whether at the national or more localized level) and
community-spirited groups to recognize their common goals of
improving the lives of senior citizens. Hopefully, too, the concept of lifelong learning can be incorporated into this discourse.
Practitioners should ensure that this is the case.

CONCLUSION

This chapter has entailed an attempt to investigate some of
the issues affecting the lives of older adults and their potential
for learning. Six issues have been selected in which older adults

have special interest in further debate and possible resolution. Their common thread has been the sense of urgency and immediacy in which members of society need to engage with older adults. In most instances I have used examples from my own cultural context to provide greater immediacy of the issue while acknowledging that slightly different complexions of the issues exist elsewhere.

CHAPTER 9

Towards a Critical
Educational Gerontology

In chapter 2 I drew together some of the strands of inquiry regarding the current state of educational gerontology. It is a diffuse field, struggling to find its academic credibility, in much the same way as adult education itself. The intent of this book has been to present some coherence to an evolving subfield which incorporates ideas and concepts from adult education/learning as well as studies of how older adults conduct their lives in a changing social world (social gerontology). In this final chapter, I argue for a critical stance to educational gerontology, how such an approach could empower older adults, and I offer an exemplar of critical educational gerontology in action, using a political economy approach. In addition, I consider issues for the future which emanate from this paradigm shift.

WHY IS A CRITICAL EDUCATIONAL
GERONTOLOGY NECESSARY?

As argued in chapter 2, the functionalist tradition of giving primary attention to the successful adjustment of individuals to the social order does not help those older adults who are marginalized with respect to resources in society through social class, gender, ethnicity, disability or some other condition. Several educational gerontologists have acknowledged the limitations of current conceptions of this field and have used critical theory as a basis for new developments (Arber & Ginn,

1995; Battersby, 1987; Battersby & Glendenning, 1992; Cusack, 2000; Phillipson, 1998, 2000).

In insightful books *Adult Education as Vocation* and *Critical Crosscurrents in Education* (1991, 1998), critical theorist Michael Collins investigates many of the taken-for-granted concepts within (adult) education and subjects them to critique. He explains how critical theory has been used by adult educators to scrutinize the instrumental and technical aspects of their roles and instead he advocates a recognition of the importance of commitment to collective social change as a basis for transformative pedagogy. He comments that "critical theory offers a way for us to understand the distortions and inequities of contemporary pedagogy" (1991, p.109) and that such an emancipatory project "necessitates a systematic disclosure and analysis of contradictions within contemporary social structures" (1998, p.66).

Within educational gerontology the incorporation of critical perspectives has been slow. As a result, the field has labored under approaches which have focussed on individual physiological and psychological functioning to the detriment of social analysis, especially from a more sociological perspective. This book has attempted to remedy this neglect and to strategically connect critical perspectives on adult learning with those on educational gerontology in a more critical positioning. As alerted in chapter 2, the purpose has been to synthesize older adults' learning with an emergent critical perspective.

In the book edited by Frank Glendenning entitled *Teaching and Learning in Later Life: Theoretical Implications*, Phillipson (2000) elaborates on three perspectives about the nature of an aging society:

1. The political economy perspective in which there is an awareness of the structural pressures and constraints affecting older people, the most obvious of which are gender relations, ethnicity and social class

2. The perspective from the humanities of contributions from scholars such as Thomas Cole and Harry Moody who sometimes combined with historians and ethicists. Their concern

was focussed on the meaning which older adults give to their daily lives in routines and relationships.

3. The biographical and narrative perspectives in gerontology. Advocates of this approach extend our knowledge through the social construction of later life.

All three perspectives share an orientation of critique of prevailing understandings within gerontology and endeavor to develop alternative approaches to understanding the processes of growing old. Phillipson (2000, p.26) notes further that:

> from all three perspectives there is a focus on the issue of empowerment, through the transformation of society (for example, the redistribution of income and wealth), or the development of new rituals and symbols to facilitate changes through the life course.

While the component of critique within critical theory is significant, it should also offer a positive direction for practitioners. It should move beyond negative critique. Hence, below I present a critical approach applied to the context of older adults as an example of how a critical theory analysis of older adults' learning can provide a way forward as a conceptual tool.

EMPOWERMENT OF OLDER ADULTS

One of the distinguishing characteristics of a critical approach to educational gerontology is the concern for "power relations" or "empowerment" of disenfranchised groups in society. The issue of empowerment (sometimes the words "emancipation" or "liberation" are used synonymously) is fundamental to older adults who are oppressed by existing social structures. Of course, being an older adult of itself does not qualify one to be an oppressed person as many older adults are financially secure and have real choices in their lives. Instead, my notion of "disempowered" older adults refers to those who do not have equitable access to resources, the attainment of which would make the quality of their lives significantly better. Usually this oppression is captured in group membership and differential access to power (e.g. through gender or cultural affiliation). Membership of that minority group bestows relatively less influence on decision-making and reduced freedom to conduct one's life with integrity.

So, what is meant by the empowerment of older adults? A traditional sense of empowerment occurs when power is shared more equitably between dominant and subordinate groups in society (Cervero & Wilson et al., 2001; Mayo, 1997). Seldom is power "handed over" in an explicit sense but is more often "negotiated" or arrested from those in positions of authority and of responsibility who are forced to share power begrudgingly (Gramsci, 1971). Sometimes, as argued by Cusack (2000, p.65), the notions of "power with" or "power to" rather than "power over" characterize the situation as one of empowerment. In her case, seniors in an educational setting in Vancouver play a significant role in setting agendas, shaping policies and planning programs and this constitutes empowerment. To me, this is empowerment in a constrained, limited sense, a "softer" form of power relations. The position that I assume as necessary for more equitable power relations between groups contesting for knowledge and resources is that which critiques social structures and advocates for subordinate groups to seek redress in a nonviolent manner. Cervero and Wilson et al. (2001) identify the fundamental issue of power as "redistributing power" rather than "the ability to get things done" but the two positions are not entirely mutually exclusive. The basic idea is to redistribute power and knowledge so that marginalized groups, such as those occupied by many older adults, can attain a fair share of resources.

Discourses Within a
Critical Educational Gerontology

A range of discourses can be used to encapsulate critical stances to educational gerontology (some described above) but it is probably fair to observe that the application of critical theory to this field is in its infancy. A significant consequence of using critical theory is to suspend our preconceptions about older adults and learning (refer to chapter 2 for the eight sub-areas of possible study), to take little for granted and to delve beneath the surface of appearances. Theories from a political economy perspective (e.g. Wangoola & Youngman, 1996), feminist positions (e.g. Ryan, 2001), cultural studies (e.g. Blaikie, 1999), postmodernism (e.g. Usher, Bryant & Johnson, 1997) and biographical narratives (e.g. Koch, Annells & Brown, 2000) all provide useful insights into the ideological and material positions of older adults. No single theory provides complete answers to questions concerning older adults and learning. What these theories can do is to alert us to new possibilities, to ask new questions.

As an exemplar of one critical theory, I am using the political economy approach to illustrate how such a perspective can illuminate the social and material conditions of older adults in which they engage in learning. This is by no means a new approach—its antecedents are in radical (Marxist) sociology—but, as the work of Phillipson (1998, 2000) has already illustrated, it has sound explanatory power in the arena of educational gerontology.

REVISITING A POLITICAL ECONOMY APPROACH

The Role of the State

The state is a major determinant of the contours of older adults' lives. In the New Zealand context (and undoubtedly elsewhere) the state's positioning with respect to aging has been to define it "primarily as an illness, to the exclusion of older people from the public sphere, and to relatively high rates of institutionalisation" (Saville-Smith, 1993, p.77). The 1898 Old Age Pensions Act, an important legislative event in the country's welfare history, marks an initial period of provision by the state but it also begins an ambiguous relationship in terms of structured dependency of older adults. In this case, as in other Western countries, it is desirable to understand the social history, social policy development and patterns of economic provision for senior citizens. In recent times under the ideology of neoliberalism, much of the "generosity" of the past has been eroded to the extent of current publicly resourced pensions. Increasingly adults have been expected to individually plan their financial circumstances for old age and not be reliant on government funding (Phillipson, 1998). The consequence of this erratic social policy is that historically different cohorts of older people have had varying levels of benefit from the state related to political and economic imperatives. There are distinct generational effects on the extent to which "retirement" is supported by the state and of individuals' capacity to meet financial costs in their old age.

Social Class

The impact on older adults of social class—defined here as a combination of accumulated financial capital and present socioeconomic status—is not consistent across countries. In the New Zealand context, the nation's beginnings were as a purported egalitarian society. The reality of the "classless society" has been quite different, with the gaps between rich and poor widening, though nothing like the huge disparities in the UK and USA. Whereas in the time of my parents' generation home ownership was a realistic option for working class people, this is no longer valid. Either young families cannot afford the deposit on a house or they now choose to spend their income on possessions other than property.

The structure of the workforce, in line with the government's desire to create more flexible and skilled workers, is changing from a heavily dependent agricultural base to one more focussed on human services (e.g. tourism). Thomson's (1999) analysis is that full-time paid work may be the privilege of a smaller core of workers around whom, at the periphery, a growing group of part-time and casual laborers operate. The notion of a person continuing on a stable career path throughout life until late adulthood is in jeopardy. People from marginalized ethnic groups, such as Maori and Pasifika, are much more prone to casual labor and uncertain family economies, thus making their third age more restricted, especially given their relative lack of higher level educational qualifications (Yates, 1996). Counterbalancing this gloomy picture, is the fact that in these collectively oriented cultures, the status of the aged is usually high and their care by younger members of the family is expected under custom.

A serious question to be answered is what impact the recent removal of compulsory retirement will have on the workforce. Will older adults increasingly stay at work as an economic necessity? Will employers adopt more liberating policies of employment to allow for more part-time work for people in their 50s, 60s and 70s? Will economic gaps between rich and poor shrink or enlarge under this regime? We await responses.

Gender

In chapter 4, I pointed to the truism that aging and gender intersect, with older age becoming increasingly feminized. Traditionally, the care of families has been the primary domain of women but in contemporary societies the range of family types and lifestyles has extended, with the result that conventional patterns of female-carer and male-provider are far less valid.

The differential experiences of women and men in retirement can, in most instances, be traced to different work, education and childrearing patterns. Men have tended to have significant changes in lifestyle, often from an instrumental to an expressive modality; women tend to continue existing living patterns, with stronger possibilities of veering towards instrumental activities. For both genders, the likelihood of volunteering is high but is quite class-based, the majority of volunteers emerging from the middle class (Caro & Bass, 1995).

Bonita (1993) explains that the social context for older

women is usually different from men's. "Distinct differences between older men and older women can be seen in marital status,
living arrangements and caretaking responsibilities" (p.195).
Further, older women often face the twin discriminations of
sexism and ageism, and because status is often linked to economic contribution in the public domain, they tend to have lifelong lower power and rewards. It is more often the position for
women that they have fewer resources, decreasing health and
mobility, loss of partners and friends and the threat of increasing dependency (ibid, p.191).

Ethnicity

In the New Zealand context, most people are European
(Pakeha), related to dominant patterns of colonization. In a
population of only four million, until recently the country was
extremely monocultural, despite the country's official position
as a bicultural nation where Maori language has higher status
under the law (it is the only official language) but English is
much more widely used. After migration of many Maori from
rural to urban environments in the 1960s and after immigration
of Pasifika peoples (mainly in Auckland) in the 1970s and more
recent Asian waves of immigrants in the 1990s, the country has
become much more multicultural, particularly in the main urban areas of the North Island. The resultant settlement modes
of various ethnic groups illustrate a patchy tapestry of occupation where certain ethnic groups buy property in "working class
areas" and others in more salubrious surroundings. In this way,
social reproduction is continued and poverty can become intergenerational.

Marginalization is experienced by Maori and Pasifika
peoples in most social institutions, including education. Social
equity programs have been introduced by government in public
institutions such as the schooling system to address historically
inequitable outcomes. For Maori, the historical alienation frequently experienced in schools and consequent underachieve-
ment has resulted in a parallel Maori-controlled system in edu-

cation being established by Maori themselves. These range from preschool language nests (*kohanga reo*) to tertiary education initiatives (*whare wananga*) where Maori language and protocol are employed as the usual mode of social interaction. In other public spheres, similar bids for self-determination have been piloted, as in alternative justice approaches. The generalization from this case is that the indigenous people have taken initiatives to try to influence their own destiny after subordination through colonization.

In the traditional Maori context the role of older adults is quite prescribed and tends to be gender specific (men as leaders in public domains; women in auxiliary roles). However, in the modern urban context much of this order breaks down, resulting in fragmentation of roles and considerable ambiguity for appropriate behavior. Often the individualistic ideology of Pakeha takes precedence over the collective ethos previously cultivated in traditional settings (Gramsci, 1971), thus leaving some older Maori with identity confusion (Erikson, 1978).

Role confusion is not restricted to Maori elders. Around the world, especially among indigenous groups, what it means to be an elder in a traditional sense is under threat. To a significant degree, this confusion is related to a global movement in which youthfulness, vitality and glamour are valued more highly than wisdom, endurance and integrity. As Blaikie comments:

> Our changing images of elderly people in the twentieth century although securely locked in history have been particularly influenced by modernity and the value systems of a modern consumer culture—The processes of modernisation and technological innovation render the skills and knowledge of older generations redundant (1999, p.347).

Some indigenous women face treble discrimination—from old age, from being indigenous and from being a woman. The issue becomes what valued knowledge can these older people pass on (raised in a very different economic and political context which emphasized collectivity) to new generations (brought up on mass consumerism and an ideology of individualism)?

IMPLICATIONS OF THIS POLITICAL
ECONOMY ANALYSIS

In general terms, this example has been concerned with the social and material conditions of older adults' lives which vary according to the political economy context i.e. according to social class, gender and ethnic factors.

There are clear implications for the state. There is still a role to play in the provision of public facilities and social welfare to ensure different sub-populations of older adults are treated fairly. Although structured dependency should be avoided, the state can foster opportunities for minorities of older adults to work together in conducive environments (including appropriate cultural settings).

From an educational perspective, social policy in New Zealand and other countries needs to be more attuned to the ongoing learning needs of people throughout life and encourage older adults in particular to pursue education opportunities as a right. Older adults in many societies, despite negative stereotyping of their capabilities, still have leadership responsibilities for which education can function as a catalyst and mode of knowledge validation.

LIFELONG LEARNING
AND JUSTICE ISSUES

The concept of lifelong learning provides a basis for arguing that learning for older adults is an essential element of living and that educational provision should be justified as a basic human right. Age should have nothing to do with one's access to education. However, there are many types of education, most of which reinforce the status quo from which older adults, especially those in the lower socioeconomic echelons and minority groups, are largely disenfranchised.

There are numerous possible educational responses to the social issues faced by older adults (such as those discussed in chapter 8). The recommended path to follow from examining the contours of educational gerontology is one which embraces a critical theory approach. Necessarily, the challenge is to move beyond the functionalist, conservative tradition of consumer-driven provision for older adults (i.e. the coping and expressive needs-based approach) to a more participatory, collaborative mode in which older adults are principal stakeholders in the purposes and outcomes of education. In addition, while they may fulfil personal needs in this process they are more importantly contributing through social action to improving the predicaments of disenfranchised older adults and to society more generally.

In the call for fundamental justice for all members of society to have an on-going education throughout life, Elmore (2000) argues for a strong moral dimension. In a liberal democracy he proposes that there is a basic right for individuals to be treated as equals (with associated respect). Further, he claims on the grounds of equal educational opportunity and of an informed citizenship (with associated rights and duties) that education for older people be available to them. The issue then becomes one of political will and the preparedness of governments to implement policy based on these moral assumptions. Given the track record of most governments, this call for justice is likely to go unheeded unless older adults themselves, sometimes in coalition with other groups in society (Alinsky, 1971; Gramsci, 1971; Mayo, 1997), assert their collective intent and mobilize for action. This is where a critical educational gerontology holds out hope for older adults.

IMPLICATIONS FOR PRACTITIONERS

As a practitioner reading this book, you may think "What do I do with this knowledge about the social context of older adults' learning"? Although there are no recipes for sure success, the following observations are made to highlight what might improve practice in working alongside senior citizens.

Critical Questioning

There is so much educators take for granted in our professional work lives. In the busyness of day-to-day demands, we often make assumptions about how others think, what their views on learning are likely to be, and their potential for further development. Our preconceptions about older adults are no exception. We need to suspend our assumptions about older people, test out our own prejudices and learn to be more self-critical in our dealings with them. As indicated in chapter 4, myths abound about how older adults pattern their lives. We do a disservice to ourselves and older adults by forming stereotypes, especially concerning of what we think they are capable, of what they can achieve, if given accurate information and encouragement. We need to remain cognizant of our own thinking and continue to question what we believe reality to be.

Going Beyond Needs Assessment

Educators are too often obsessed with the idea of assessing the learning needs of subgroups of the population, including older adults, in an instrumental fashion. Although quick-fix instruments of needs analysis based on psychological models of human behavior continue to provide glimpses of what older adults "need", there is no substitute for gaining more in-depth knowledge of individuals' social lives and of groups or institutions to which they belong. Essentially, humans are social animals, not freed from prevailing political and cultural configurations of which they are part. We should develop greater understanding of minority group members through situational analysis in ways to honor their integrity and self-determination.

Linked to the imperative to go beyond a needs-based approach to comprehend seniors' lives is the scope to develop a fuller situational analysis to include social structures (age, gender, social class, ethnicity, geographical location) and the cultural heritage of particular groups (Cervero & Wilson et al., 2001). For example, when working with a Latino group if from another ethnic group, we should be more aware and knowledgeable of their cultural dynamics and special interests. If necessary, we should work through intermediaries who have first-hand experience of successfully negotiating educational opportunity for such a group. The development of a partnership with specific groups, where trust has developed over time, can bring benefits to both parties.

Providers Accepting Responsibility

One latent theme in this book has been the heterogeneity of older adults and the range of public responses to their varied situations in a time of dramatic social change in contemporary society (as illustrated in chapters 4 and 8). We cannot afford to be complacent and work only with those who have already prospered from the education service (usually the white middle-class) but extend provision of educational opportunity to all sectors of the society in which we live. To this end, educational providers should adopt a coherent policy of where they stand ideologically and practically to different sectors of the community, in this case, older adults and subsets of older learners. If a provider is publicly funded there is a moral obligation to represent the full interests of that community, especially those traditionally disenfranchised from participation. Educators in public institutions should develop clear objectives of how to more actively engage older citizens in the formulation, implementation and evaluation of educational provision (Caffarella, 2001).

Strategic Advocacy

The marginalization of many older adults restricts their capacity to be fully human (Moody, 1976) and we should advocate more for their greater involvement in public life. Many older adults are quite capable of their own advocacy so we need to avoid unnecessary patronizing of them. They can exercise their own agency. More effective advocacy may involve our membership of organizations in which older adults are in the majority (an indirect influence) or it may entail cooperating with institutions representing the interests of older adults (e.g. Age Concern; Senior Citizens Clubs). Not only do older adults tend to benefit in terms of heightened self-esteem and health but the broader society also benefits through increased volunteering activity and the strengthening of social institutions.

At a political level, the influence of Grey Power and other older adults' advocacy groups has proven the potential for direct persuasion to effect change when warranted. Some adult educators from a more radical framework would see themselves aligned to advocacy groups which are endeavoring to change public policy and societal discrimination against older citizens (Cusack, 2000). However, most practitioners are part of the mainstream of society and are unlikely to adopt an extremist position. For them, intelligent engagement with older adults to assist them to achieve their life goals is a realistic alternative.

REFERENCES

Alinsky, S. (1971). *Rules for Radicals: A Pragmatic Primer for Realistic Radicals*. New York: Vintage Books.

Althusser, L (1972). *Lenin and Philosophy and Other Essays*. New York: Monthly Review.

Arber, S. & Ginn, J. (Eds). (1995). *Connecting Gender and Ageing: A Sociological Approach*. Buckingham: Open University Press.

Arsenault, N., Anderson, G. & Swedburg, R. (1998). Understanding Older Adults in Education: Decision-making and Elderhostel, *Educational Gerontology*, vol. 24, no.2, pp.101–114.

Australian Senate Standing Committee on Employment, Education and Training (1991). *Come in Cinderella: The Emergence of Adult and Community Education*. Canberra: Senate Publications Unit, Parliament of the Commonwealth of Australia.

Battersby, D. (1987). From Andragogy to Gerogogy, *Journal of Educational Geronotogy*, vol.2, no.12, pp.4–10.

Battersby, D. & Glendenning, F. (1992). Reconstructing Education for Older Adults: An Elaboration of the Statement of First Principles, *Australian Journal of Adult and Community Education*, vol.32, no.2, pp.115–121.

Beatty, P. T. & Wolf, M. A. (1996). *Connecting with Older Adults: Educational Responses and Approaches*. Malabar, FL: Krieger.

Becker, H. (1963). *Outsiders*. Oxford: Free Press.

Belenky, M.F, Clinchy, B. M., Goldberger, N. R., & Tarule, J. M. (1986). *Women's Ways of Knowing: The Development of Self, Voice and Mind*. New York: Basic Books.

Benseman, J. (1980). *The Assessment and Meeting of Needs in Continuing Education*. Stockholm Institute of Education: Department of Educational Research.

Benseman, J. (1996). Participation in the Fourth Sector. In Benseman, J., Findsen, B. & Scott, M. (Eds.), *The Fourth Sector: Adult and Community Education in Aotearoa/New Zealand*. Palmerston North: Dunmore Press.

Berger, P. L. & Berger, B. (1976). *Sociology: A Biographical Approach*. Harmondsworth: Penguin.

Berger, P. & Luckmann, T. (1991). *The Social Construction of Reality: A Treatise in the Sociology of Knowledge*, Harmondsworth: Penguin.

Biggs, S. (1993). *Understanding Ageing: Images, Attitudes and Professional Practice*. Buckingham: Open University Press.

Blackledge, D. & Hunt, B. (1985). *Sociological Interpretations of Education*. London: Croom Helm.

Blaikie, A. (1999). *Ageing and Popular Culture*. Cambridge University Press.

Blaxter, L. & Tight, M. (1995). Life Transitions and Educational Participation by Adults, *International Journal of Lifelong Education*, vo.14, no.3, pp.231–246.

Boone, E. J. (1985). *Developing Programs in Adult Education*. Englewood Cliffs, NJ: Prentice Hall.

Bond, J., Coleman, P., & Peace, S. (Eds.). (1998). *Ageing in Society: An Introduction to Social Gerontology* (2nd ed.). London: Sage.

Bonita, R. (1993). Older Women: A Growing Force. Chapter 8 in Koopman-Boyden, P. *New Zealand's Ageing Society: The Implications*. Wellington: Daphne Brasell Associates Press, pp.189–212.

Borowski, A., Encel, S. & Ozanne, E. (Eds.). (1997). *Ageing and Social Policy in Australia*. Cambridge: Cambridge University Press.

Boshier, R. (1978). Adult Education Program Planning and Instructional Design, *Continuing Education in New Zealand*, vol. 10, no.1, May, pp.33–50.

Boshier, R. (1980). *Towards a Learning Society*. Vancouver: Learning-Press.

Boud, D. & Miller, N. (Eds.). (1996). *Working with Experience: Animating Learning*. New York: Routledge.

Bourdieu, P. (1974). The School as a Conservative Force. In Eggleston, J. (Ed.), *Contemporary Research in the Sociology of Education*. London: Metheuen.

Brookfield, S. (1986). *Understanding and Facilitating Adult Learning*. San Francisco: Jossey-Bass.

Brookfield, S. (1987). *Developing Critical Thinkers*. San Francisco: Jossey-Bass.

Bury, M. (1995). Ageing, Gender and Sociological Theory. In Arber, S.

& Ginn, G. (Eds.), *Connecting Gender and Ageing*. Buckingham: Oxford University Press.

Butler, R. N. (1982). Successful Aging and the Role of Life Review. In S. H. Zarit (Ed), *Readings in Aging and Death: Contemporary Perspectives*. (2nd ed.) pp.20–26. New York: Harper & Row.

Bytheway, B. (1995). *Ageism*. Buckingham: Open University Press.

Caffarella, R. S. (2001). *Planning Programs for Adult Learners: A Practical Guide for Educators, Trainers, and Staff Developers* (2nd ed.). San Francisco: Jossey-Bass.

Carlton, S. & Soulsby, J. (1999). *Learning to Grow Older and Bolder: A Policy Discussion Paper on Learning in Later Life*. Leicester, England: The National Institute of Adult Continuing Education.

Carmin, C. (1988). *Issues on Research on Mentoring: Definitional and Methodological*, International Journal of Mentoring, vol. 2, no.2, pp.9–13.

Caro, F. G. & Bass, S. A. (1995). Increasing Volunteering Among Older People. Chapter 4 in Caro, F. G. & Scott, A. *Older and Active: How Americans over 55 are Contributing to Society*. New Haven, CT: Yale University Press, pp.71–96.

Cervero, R. M. & Wilson, A. L. & Associates (2001). *Power in Practice: Adult Education and the Struggle for Knowledge and Power in Society*. San Francisco: Jossey-Bass.

Chen, Y. & Persson, A. (2002). Internet Use among Young and Older Adults: Relation to Psychological Well-Being, *Educational Gerontology*, vol.28, pp.731–744.

Clark, F., Heller, A. F., Rafman, C. & Walker, J. (1997). Peer Learning: A Popular Model for Seniors Education, *Educational Gerontology*, vol. 23, no.8, pp.751–762.

Clark, M. M. & Anderson, B. (1967). *Culture and Aging: An Anthropological Study of Older Americans*. Springfield, IL: Charles C Thomas.

Cody, M. J., Dunn, D., Hoppin, S. & Wendt, P. (1999). Silver Surfers: Training and Evaluating Internet Use among Older Adult learners, *Communication Education*, vol.48, no.4, pp.269–286.

Collins, M. (1991). *Adult Education as Vocation*. Routledge: London.

Collins, M. (1998). *Critical Crosscurrents in Education*. Malabar, FL: Krieger.

Cross, P. (1981). *Adults as Learners*. San Francisco: Jossey-Bass.

Cusack, S. (2000). Critical Educational Gerontology and the Imperative to Empower. Chapter 6 in Glendenning, F. (Ed.), *Teaching and*

Learning in Later life: Theoretical Implications. Aldershot: Ashgate Publishers, pp.61–76.

Darkenwald, G. G. & Merriam, S. B. (1982). *Adult Education: Foundations of Practice.* New York: Harper Row.

Denzin, N. (1988). *Interpretive Biography.* Newbury Park: Sage.

Dewey, J. (1938). *Experience and Education.* New York: Collier Books.

Drewery, W. (1991) Adult Development: Infant with Unexpected Potential. In Morss, J. & Linzey, T. (Eds.), *Growing up: The politics of human learning.* Auckland: Longman Paul.

Elderhostel (2003). Facts About the Elderhostel Institute Network. Taken from *www.elderhostel.org/Ein/factsheet.asp* on 21 May 2003.

Elias, J. L. & Merriam, S. B. (1995). *Philosophical Foundations of Adult Education* (2nd ed.). Malabar, FL: Krieger.

Elmore, R. (2000). Education for Older People: The Moral Dimension. Chapter 5 in Glendenning, F. (Ed.). (2000). *Teaching and Learning in Later Life: Theoretical Implications.* Aldershot: Ashgate, pp.49–60.

Erikson, E. H. (1978). *Adulthood.* New York: Norton.

Estes, C. L. (1991). The New Political Economy of Aging: Introduction and Critique. Chapter 2 in Minkler, M. & Estes, C. L. (Eds.), *Critical Perspectives on Aging.* Amilyrike, NJ: Bayward, pp.19–36.

Estes, C. (1998). Critical Gerontology and the New Political Economy of Aging. In Minkler, C. & Estes, C. (Eds.), *Critical Gerontology: Perspectives from Political and Moral Economy.* New York: Baywood.

Evans, L. & Abbott, I. (1998). *Teaching and Learning in Higher Education.* London: Cassell.

Faure, E. et al. (1972). *Learning to Be.* Paris: UNESCO.

Findsen, B. (1996). Developing Educational Programmes for Adults. In Benseman, J., Findsen, B. & Scott, M. (Eds.), *The Fourth Sector: Adult and Community Education in Aotearoa New Zealand.* Palmerston North: Dunmore Press, pp.263–273.

Findsen, B. (1998). Freire as an Adult Educator: An International Perspective. *The New Zealand Journal of Adult Learning*, vol. 26, no.1, pp.9–22.

Findsen, B. (1999a). Freire and Adult Education: Principles and Practice. In Roberts, P. (Ed.), *Paulo Freire, Politics and Pedagogy: Reflections from Aotearoa New Zealand.* Palmerston North: Palmerston North, pp.71–82.

Findsen, B. (1999b). Working Alongside Older Adults: Challenges for Adult Educators, *Perspectives in Social Work.* Vol. 14, no.2, pp.18–27.

Findsen, B. (2001). Older Adults' Access to Higher Education in New

Zealand, *Journal of Access and Credit Studies*, vol. 3, no.2, Winter 2001–2002, pp.118–129.

Fingeret, A. (1983). Social Network: A New Perspective on Independence and Illiterate Adults. *Adult Education Quarterly*, vol. 33, no.3, pp.133–146.

Fisher, J. C. (1993). A Framework for Describing Developmental Change Among Older Adults, *Adult Education Quarterly*, vol.43, no.2, pp.76–89.

Fisher, J. C. & Wolf, M. A. (Eds.). (1998). *Using Learning to Meet the Challenges of Older Adulthood*. New Directions for Adult and Continuing Education. No.77, Spring. San Francisco: Jossey-Bass.

Fox, S., Rainie, L., Larsen, E., Horrigan, J., Lenhart, A., Spooner, T. & Carter, C. (2001) Wired Seniors: A Fervent Few, Inspired by Family Ties Http://www.pewinternet.org/reports/pdfs/Pip_Wired_Seniors_Report.pdf

Freire, P. (1984). *Pedagogy of the Oppressed*. New York: Continuum.

Fryer, R. (1997). *Learning for the Twenty-First Century: First Report of the National Advisory Group for Continuing Education and Lifelong Learning*. London: NAGCELL.

Gatt-Fly. (1996). *Ah-hah! A New Approach to Popular Education*. (2nd ed.) Toronto, Canada: Between the Lines.

Gaventa, J. (1980). *Power and Powerlessness: Quiescence and Rebellion in an Appalachian Valley*. Chicago: University of Illinois Press.

Gerson, K.(1985). *Hard Choices: How Women Decide about Work, Career, and Motherhood*. Berkeley & Los Angeles: University of California Press.

Giroux, H. A. (Dec.1979), Toward a New Sociology of the Curriculum, *Educational Leadership*, pp.248–253.

Glass, J. C. (1996). Factors Affecting Learning in Older Adults, *Educational Gerontology*, vol.22, pp.359–372.

Glendenning, F. (1985). (Ed.). *Educational Gerontology: International Perspectives*. London: Croom Helm.

Glendenning, F. & Battersby, D. (1990). Why We Need Educational Gerontology and Education for Older Adults: A Statement of First Principles. Chapter 17 in Glendenning, F. & Percy, K. (Eds.), *Ageing, Education and Society: Readings in Educational Gerontology*. Association for Educational Gerontology: University of Keele, pp.219–232.

Glendenning, F. & Percy, K. (Eds.). (1990). *Ageing, Education and Society: Readings in Educational Gerontology*. Association for Educational Gerontology: University of Keele.

Glendenning, F. & Battersby, D. (1992). Reconstructing Education for Older Adults: An Elaboration of the Statement of First Principles, *Australian Journal of Adult and Community Education*, vol.32, no.2, July, pp.115–121.

Glendenning, F. (Ed.). (2000). *Teaching and Learning in Later Life: Theoretical Implications*. Aldershot: Ashgate.

Goff, P. (1982). *Learning for Life: Two*. Wellington: Government Printer.

Goleman, D. (1995). *Emotional Intelligence*. London: Bloomsbury.

Gramsci, A. (1971). *The Prison Notebooks*. London: Lawrence & Wishart.

Green, T. (1993). Institutional Care, Community Services and the Family. Chapter 7 in Koopman-Boyden, P. *New Zealand's Ageing Society: The Implications*. Wellington: Daphne Brasell Associates Press, pp.149–186.

Guttman, D. (1975). Parenthood: A Key to the Comparative Study of the Life Cycle. In Datan, N. & Ginsberg, L. (Eds.), *Life-Span Developmental Psychology: Normative Life Crises*. New York: Simon & Schuster.

Guttman, D. L. (1987). *Reclaimed Powers*. New York: Basic Books.

Havighurst, R. J. (1953). *Human Development and Education*. New York: Longmans, Green.

Havighurst, R. J. (1972). *Developmental Tasks and Education* (3rd ed.). New York: McKay.

Henretta, J. C. (1994). Social Structure and Age-Based Careers. Chapter 3 in Riley, M. W., Kahn, R. L. & Foner, A (Eds.), *Age and Structural Lag*. New York: Wiley, pp.57–79.

Heppner, H. (1996). 'Extending the Boundaries of Our Thinking: The Need and Rationale for Learning Opportunities in Later Life'. In *Access* (Critical Perspectives on Cultural and Policy Studies in Education), vol.15, no.2, pp.38–52.

Hiemstra, R. (1976). The Older Adults Learning Projects, *Educational Gerontology*, vol.1, pp.331–341.

Hiemstra, R. (1998). From Whence Have We Come? The First Twenty-Five Years of Educational Gerontology. Chapter 1 in Fisher, J. C. & Wolf, M. A. (Eds.), *Using Learning to Meet the Challenges of Older Adulthood*. New Directions for Adult and Continuing Education. No.77, Spring. San Francisco: Jossey-Bass, pp.5–14.

Horton, M., Kohl, J. & Kohl, H. (1990). *The Long Haul: An Autobiography*. New York: Doubleday.

Houle, C. O. (1961). *The Inquiring Mind*. Madison: University of Wisconsin Press.

Illich, I. (1973). *Deschooling Society*. Harmondsworth: Penguin.

Ingrisch, D. (1995). Conformity and Resistance as Women Age. Chapter 4 in Arber, S. & Ginn, J. (Eds.), *Connecting Gender and Ageing: A Sociological Approach*. Buckingham: Open University Press, pp.42–55.

James, D. (1990). Striving to Preserve Identity: A Biomedical Approach. Chapter 8 in Glendenning, F. & Percy, K. (Eds.), *Ageing, Education and Society: Readings in Educational Gerontology*. Association for Educational Gerontology: Centre for Social Gerontology, University of Keele, pp.123–130.

Jarvis, P. (1985). *Sociological Perspectives on Lifelong Education and Lifelong Learning*. Athens: Department of Adult Education, University of Georgia.

Jarvis, P. (2001). *Learning in Later Life: An Introduction for Educators and Carers*. London: Kogan Page.

Jerrome, D. (1998). Intimate Relationships. Chapter 10 in Bond, J., Coleman, P., & Peace, S. (Eds.), *Ageing in Society: An Introduction to Social Gerontology*. (2nd ed.) London: Sage Publications, pp.226–254.

Johnstone, J. W.C & Rivera, R. J. (1965). *Volunteers for Learning: A Study of the Educational Pursuits of Adults*. Hawthorne, New York: Aldine.

Kelsey, J. (1999). *Reclaiming the Future: New Zealand and the Global Economy*. Wellington: Bridget Williams Books.

Kennedy, H. (1997). *Learning Works: Widening Participation in Further Education*. (Kennedy Report). Coventry: Further Education Funding Council.

Kirkwood, G & Kirkwood, C. (1989). *Living Adult Education: Freire in Scotland*. Milton Keynes: SIACE and the Open University.

Koch, T., Annells, M. & Brown, M. (2000). *Still Doing: Twelve Men talk About Aging*. South Australia: Wakefield Press.

Kolb, D. A. (1984). *Experiential Learning: Experience as the Source of Learning and Development*. Englewood Cliffs, NJ: Prentice Hall.

Koopman-Boyden, P. (1993). *New Zealand's Ageing Society: The Implications*. Wellington: Daphne Brasell Associates Press.

Knowles, M. S. (1980). *The Modern Practice of Adult Education*. New York: Adult Education Company.

Knowles, M. S. and Associates (1984). *Andragogy in Action: Applying Modern Principles of Adult Learning*. San Francisco: Jossey-Bass.

Kubler-Ross, E. (1970). *On Death and Dying*. London: Tavistock.

Labouvie-Vief, G. (1984). Logic and Self-regulation from Youth to Maturity: A Model. In Commons, M. L., Richards, F. A., & Armon,

C. (Eds.), *Beyond Formal Operations: Late Adolescence and Adult Cognitive Development*. New York: Praeger.

Lamdin, L & Fugate, M. (1997). *Elderlearning: New Frontier in an Aging Society*. American Council on Education: Oryx Press.

Laslett, P. (1989). *A Fresh Map of Life: The Emergence of the Third Age*. London: Weidenfeld and Nicholson.

Levinson, D. J., Darrow, C. N., Klein, E. B., Levinson, M. H. & McGee, B. (1978). *The Seasons of a Man's Life*. New York: Ballantine.

Lowy, L. & O'Connor, D. (1986). *Why Education in the Later Years?* New York: D. C. Heath.

McClusky, H. Y. (1974). Education for Aging: The Scope of the Field and Perspectives for the Future. In Grabowski, S. and Mason, W. D. (Eds.), *Learning for Aging*. Washington, D.C.: Adult Education Association of the USA.

McGivney, V. (1991). *Education's for Other People: Access to Education for Non-Participant Adults*. Leicester: NIACE.

McGivney, V. (1996). *Staying on or Leaving the Course*. Leicester: NIACE.

McGivney, V. (1999). *Informal Learning in the Community: A Trigger for Change and Development*. Leicester: NIACE.

Maaka, R. (1993). Te Ao o te Pakeketanga: The World of the Aged. Chapter 9 in Koopman-Boyden, P. (1993). *New Zealand's Ageing Society: The Implications*. Wellington: Daphne Brasell Associates Press, pp.213–229.

Manheimer, R. J. (1998). The Promise and Politics of Older Adult Education, *Research on Aging*, vol.20, no.4, pp.391–415.

May, H. (1990). Growth and Change in the Early Childhood Services: A Story of Political Conservatism, Growth and Constraint. In Middleton, S., Codd, J. & Jones, A. (Eds.), *New Zealand Education Policy Today*. Wellington: Allen & Unwin, pp.94–109.

Mayo, M. (1997). *Imagining Tomorrow: Adult Education for Transformation*. Leicester: NIACE.

Meighan, R. (1981). *A Sociology of Educating*. London: Holt, Rinehart & Winston.

Merriam, S. B. (1984). *Adult Development: Implications for Adult Education*. Columbus, Ohio: ERIC Clearinghouse for Adult, Career and Vocational Education at Ohio State University.

Merriam, S. (1985). Reminiscence and Life Review: the Potential for Educational Intervention. In Sherron, R. & Lumsden, B. (Eds.), *Introduction to Educational Gerontology* (2nd ed.), Washington: Hemisphere.

Merriam, S. B. & Caffarella, R. S. (1999). *Learning in Adulthood: A Comprehensive Guide* (2nd ed.). San Francisco: Jossey-Bass.

Merriam, S. B. & Clark, M. C. (1991). *Lifelines: Patterns of Work, Love and Learning in Adulthood.* San Francisco: Jossey-Bass.

Mezirow, J. (1981). A Critical Theory of Adult Learning and Education, *Adult Education*, vol.32, no.1, pp.3–27.

Mezirow, J. (1991). *Transformative Dimensions of Adult Learning.* San Francisco: Jossey-Bass.

Mills, C. W. (1959). *The Sociological Imagination.* London: Oxford University Press.

Ministry of Education. (1996). Adult Literacy in New Zealand: Results from the International Adult literacy Survey. Wellington.

Moody, H. R. (1976). Philosophical Presuppositions of Education for Old Age, *Educational Gerontology*, vol.1, pp.1–16.

Morell, R. W., Mayhorn, C. B. & Bennett, J. (2000). A Survey of World Wide Web Use in Middle-Aged and Older Adults, *Human Factors*, vol.42, no.2, Summer, pp.175–182.

Morstain, B. R. & Smart, J. C. (1974) Reasons for Participation in Adult Education Course: A Multivariate Analysis of Group Differences, *Adult Education*, vol.24, no.2, pp.83–98.

Naisbitt, J. (1984). *Megatrends*, New York: Warner Books.

Namazi, K. H. & McClintic, M. (2003). Computer Use among Elderly Persons in Long-Term Care Facilities, *Educational Gerontology*, vol.29, 535–550.

National Committee of Enquiry into Higher Education (1997). *Higher Education in the Learning Society.* London: NCIHE.

National Institute of Adult Continuing Education (NIACE) (1993). The Learning Imperative: National Education and Training Targets and Adult Learners.

Neugarten, B. (1976) Time, Age and the Life Cycle. *American Journal of Psychiatry*, vol.136, pp.887–893.

Paterson, R. W. K. (1979). *Values, Education and the Adult.* London: Routledge & Kegan Paul.

Pearce, S. D. (1991). Toward Understanding the Participation of Older Adults in Continuing Education, *Educational Gerontology*, vol.17, pp.451–464.

Peterson, D. A. (1980). Who Are the Educational Gerontologists? *Educational Gerontology*, vol.5, pp.65–77.

Phillipson, C. (1998). *Reconstructing Old Age: New Agendas in Social Theory and Practice.* London: Sage.

Phillipson, C. (2000). Critical Educational Gerontology: Relationships and Future Developments. Chapter 3 in Glendenning, F. (Ed.).

Teaching and Learning in Later Life: Theoretical Implications. Aldershot: Ashgate, pp.25–38.

Pong, R. W. (1998). Ageing as a Resource: Lessons Learned from an Emerging Retirement Community. In Ng, S. H., A. Weatherall, J. H. Liu and C. S. F. Loong (Eds.), *Ages Ahead: Promoting Intergenerational Relationships.* Wellington, N. Z.: Victoria University Press, pp.25–39.

Ramsden, P. (1992). *Learning to Teach in Higher Education.* London: Routledge.

Riegel, K. F. (1976). The Dialectics of Human Development, *American Psychologist*, vol. 31, pp.689–700.

Riley, M. & Riley, M. (1994). Structural Lag: Past and Future. Chapter 1 in Riley, M. W., Kahn, R. L. & Foner, A. (Eds.), *Age and Structural Lag.* New York: Wiley, pp.15–36.

Rockhill, K. (1982). Researching Participation in Adult Education: The Potential of the Qualitative Perspective, *Adult Education*, vol.33, no.1, pp.3–19.

Rogers, C. R. (1983). *Freedom to Learn for the 80s.* Columbus, OH: Merrill.

Rogers, E. (1983). *The Diffusion of Innovations* (2nd ed.). New York: Free Press.

Ryan, A. B. (2001). *Feminist Ways of Knowing: Towards Theorising the Person for Radical Adult Education.* Leicester: NIACE.

Sargent, N. et al. (1997). *The Learning Divide: A Study of Participation in Adult Learning in the United Kingdom.* Leicester: NIACE.

Saville-Smith, K. (1993). The State and the Social Construction of Aging. In Koopman-Boyden, P. (Ed.), *New Zealand's Ageing Society: The Implications.* Wellington: Daphne Brasell Associates Press.

Schuller, T. & Bostyn, A. M. (1992). *Learning: Education, Training and Information in the Third Age.* Carnegie Inquiry into the Third Age. Research Paper, no.3. Dunfermline: Carnegie UK Trust.

Sheared, V. & Sissel, P. A. (2001). *Making Space: Merging Theory and Practice in Adult Education.* Westport, CT: Bergin & Garvey.

Sheehy, G. (1995). *New Passages: Mapping Your Life Across Time.* New York: Random House.

Shor, I. (1980). *Critical Teaching and Everyday Life.* Montreal: Black Rose Books.

Smelser, N. J. & Erikson, E. H. (Eds) (1980). *Themes of Work and Love in Adulthood.* Cambridge, MA: Harvard University Press.

Smith, R. M. and Associates (1990). *Learning to Learn Across the Life Span.* San Francisco: Jossey-Bass.

Stuart, M. (2000). Beyond Rhetoric: Reclaiming a Radical Agenda for Active Participation in Higher Education. Chapter 2 in Thompson, J. (Ed.), *Stretching the Academy: The Politics and Practice of Widening Participation in Higher Education*. Leicester: NIACE, pp.23–35.

Swindell, R. (1997). U3As in Australia and New Zealand: Their Value to the Wider Community and New Directions for Future Developments, *International Journal of Lifelong Education*, vol.16, no.6, pp.474–409.

Swindell, R. (1999). New Directions, Opportunities and Challenges for New Zealand U3As, *New Zealand Journal of Adult Learning*, vol.27, no.1, pp.41–57.

Tennant. M. (1988). *Psychology and Adult Learning*. New York: Routledge.

Thompson, J. (1980). (Ed.). *Adult Education for a Change*. London: Hutchinson.

Thompson, J. (1983). *Learning Liberation: Women's Responses to Men's Education*. London: Croom Helm.

Thomson, D. (1999). The Ageing Workforce in the New Millenium: Benefit or Burden? Public Lecture Delivered at Maidment Theatre, University of Auckland, 27 July.

Timmermann, S. (1998). The Role of Information Technology in Older Adult Learning. Chapter 6 in Fisher, J. C. & Wolf, M. A. (Eds.), *Using Learning to Meet the Challenges of Older Adulthood*. New Directions for Adult and Continuing Education. No.77, Spring. San Francisco: Jossey-Bass, pp.61–72.

Tobias, R. (1996) What Do Adult and Community Educators Share in Common? Chapter 2 in Benseman, J., Findsen, B. & Scott, M. (Eds.), *The Fourth Sector: Adult and Community Education in Aotearoa/New Zealand*. Palmerston North: Dunmore Press, pp.38–64.

Tobias, R. (2001). Do We Have a "Great Divide" in Lifelong Learning? Trends in Educational Participation by Adults in Aotearoa New Zealand, 1977–1996. Paper Presented at the Annual Conference of the New Zealand Association for Research in Education, December. Christchurch.

Toffler, A. (1980). *The Third Wave*. London: William Collins Sons.

Tough, A. (1971). *The Adults' Learning Projects: A Fresh Approach to Theory and Practice in Adult Learning*. Toronto: Ontario Institute for Studies in Education.

Tough, A. (1979). *The Adults' Learning Projects: A Fresh Approach to Theory and Practice in Adult Learning* (2nd ed.). Toronto: Ontario Institute for Studies in Education.

Usher, R., Bryant, I. & Johnston, R. (1997). *Adult Education and the*

Postmodern Challenge: Learning Beyond the Limits. New York: Routledge.

Walker, J. (1990). The Politics of Provision and Participation. Chapter 6 in Glendenning, F. & Percy, K. (Eds.), *Ageing, Education and Society: Readings in Educational Gerontology.* Association for Educational Gerontology: Centre for Social Gerontology, University of Keele, pp.96–113.

Wangoola, P. & Youngman, F. (1996). (Eds). *Towards a Transformative Political Economy of Adult Education: Theoretical and Practical Challenges.* De Kalb: LEPS Press, Northern Illinois University.

White, R., Kahn, R. & Foner, A. (1994). *Age and Structural Lag.* New York: Wiley.

Williamson, A. (2000). Gender Differences in Older Adults' Participation in Learning: Viewpoints and Experiences of Learners in the University of the Third Age (U3A), *Educational Gerontology*, vol.26, pp.49–66.

Withnall, A. & Percy, K. (1994). *Good Practice in Education and Training of Older Adults.* Aldershot: Ashgate.

Withnall, A. (2000). The Debate Continues: Integrating Educational Gerontology with Lifelong Learning. Chapter 8 in Glendenning, F. (Ed.) *Teaching and Learning in Later Life: Theoretical Implications.* Aldershot: Ashgate., pp.87–98.

Wolf, M. A. (1998). New Approaches to the Education of Older Adults. Chapter 2 in Fisher, J. C. & Wolf, M. A. (Eds.), *Using Learning to Meet the Challenges of Older Adulthood.* New Directions for Adult and Continuing Education. No.77, Spring, pp.15–26.

Yates, B. (1996). Striving for Tino Rangtiratanga. In Benseman, B., Findsen, B. & Scott, M. (Eds.), *The Fourth Sector: Adult and Community Education in Aotearoa/New Zealand.* Palmerston North: Dunmore Press, pp.95–111.

INDEX